W9-BDL-424

Style, Sex, & Substance

10 Catholic Women Consider the Things That Really Matter

Hallie Lord, Editor

Our Sunday Visitor Publishing Division
Our Sunday Visitor, Inc.
Huntington, Indiana 46750

Copyright © 2012 by Hallie Lord. Published 2012.

17 16 15 14 13 12   1 2 3 4 5 6 7 8 9

ISBN: 978-1-61278-572-1 (Inventory No. T1270)

eISBN: 978-1-61278-209-6

LCCN: 2012930597

Cover design by Lindsey Riesen
Cover art: Shutterstock
Interior design by M. Urgo

PRINTED IN THE UNITED STATES OF AMERICA

Table of Contents

Introduction   5

Chapter 1. **How I Fell Out of My Minivan and
Found Myself** — Jennifer Fulwiler   13

Chapter 2. **Style: Balance, Beauty, and You** — Hallie Lord   25

Chapter 3. **God and Godiva** — Karen Edmisten   39

Chapter 4. **Sex, Passion, and Purity** — Elizabeth Duffy   57

Chapter 5. **Single and Seeking God's Plan** — Anna Mitchell   75

Chapter 6. **What Works for You?** — Rebecca Ryskind Teti   87

Chapter 7. **Fruitful Friendship** — Rachel Balducci   101

Chapter 8. **We Said Yes** — Danielle Bean   117

Chapter 9. **Receiving, Creating, and Letting Go:
Motherhood in Body and Soul** — Simcha Fisher   135

Chapter 10. **Plugging In and Embracing Discipleship In the
Twenty-First Century** — Barbara R. Nicolosi   151

Afterword   171

Acknowledgements   174

Notes   175

I dedicate this book to Mary,
the Mother of Mercy,
who is my life, my sweetness,
and my hope.

INTRODUCTION

Hallie Lord

Somewhere between intent and delivery, something often goes awry when I try to play hostess. At the moment, for example, I'm eager to introduce you to the immensely talented women who contributed to this book. But then I recall Bridget Jones, the hapless publicist for a publishing company and an awkward hostess. You may remember the scene in the movie *Bridget Jones's Diary* in which Bridget, hosting a book launch attended by several prominent writers, causes a minor scandal by lavishing praise upon one author at the expense of the others.

She stands in front of a microphone that refuses to turn on and yells to the crowd:

> Ladies and gentlemen, welcome to the launch of *Kafka's Motorbike* — the greatest book of our time! Obviously except for your books, Mr. Rushdie, which are also very good. And Lord Archer! Yours ... aren't bad ... either. Anyway, what I mean is ... uh ... welcome, ladies and gentlemen. Thank you for coming to the launch of one of the top thirty books of all time anyway ... at least.

It would be just like me to channel Bridget as I introduce you to our authors:

"First up, Jennifer Fulwiler, hands down the most talented writer of our generation. Well, except for Danielle Bean — also the number one writer of our generation. And Simcha Fisher! Now she has no rival...."

You can see how this gets problematic. The truth is that all these women *wow* me with their unique voices and insights. I couldn't possibly pick a favorite. And I can't possibly do them justice in my own words. Instead, I think I'll let them introduce themselves. I've taken a quote from their blog writing or books or elsewhere that captures the spirit of the women so that you can meet them on their own turf, so to speak. I hope these samples whet your appetite for the chapters to come.

———————◆►✕◄◆———————

The always entertaining **Jennifer Fulwiler** is a former atheist who blogs at conversiondiary.com. This excerpt from her blog post captures a conversation we had when I was acting as her stylist for my business as a personal shopper:

> Let me just say [Jen begins]: If you ever want to get a gauge of how neurotic, issue-riddled, and/or bizarre you really are, schedule a consultation with a personal shopper.
>
> [Midway through the appointment] we took a break while I went to relieve my babysitter (and Hallie probably went to pour herself something strong to drink). When we resumed, she tried a different angle.
>
> "I found some beautiful earrings. If we get a shirt that –"
>
> "My earrings are stuck in my ears."
>
> Stunned silence. "What?"
>
> "I got incredibly tight backs to keep my diamond studs from falling out, but now they won't come off. Do I

risk breaking the earrings to get them off with pliers? I haven't decided what to do about it. I need to analyze it some more."

"So, umm, wow. How long have the earrings been stuck?"

"Five years."

———◆◆▶◀◆◆———

Danielle Bean, editor-in-chief of *Catholic Digest* magazine and mother of eight, has a gift for tackling highly emotional issues with gentleness and grace. You think you've picked up a bit of light reading, but in between tales of dishes, diapers, and dates with her husband, you realize that she's hit you between the eyes with profound insight:

My husband and I are madly in love.

I feel the need to announce this publicly because, on the surface, it can be hard to tell sometimes.

Besides the challenges of daily drudgery, we have some particularly less-than-grace-filled moments as well. We sometimes engage in shouting matches about my driving skills, or lack thereof. And his social graces, or lack thereof. We occasionally give one another the cold shoulder for scandalous lengths of time over the tone one of us used when making that comment about that thing that happened the other day....

The encouraging thing about the vocation of marriage, however, is that when we fall short of our ideals, we usually get another chance.... Did you mess up that challenge? No worries. Another one is surely on its way.

Rachel Balducci, blogger and author of *How Do You Tuck in a Superhero*, is the mother of one sweet little girl and five "wild and crazy boys." Her humorous tales of "Life with Boys" never fail to comfort those of us down in the trenches with her:

> Several years ago, around Augie's second birthday, I got a phone call that would change my life.
>
> "Did you know," said my friend on the other end, "that all four of your boys are standing on the top of your truck beating it with bats?"
>
> I think I've mentioned this phone call before, how the truck belonged to Paul's dad, and the boys were, as my friend informed me, standing on the roof wielding plastic bats. That phone call signaled a new chapter in my life titled "Oh My Goodness: Life with Boys," the chapter in which I still live.

Simcha Fisher is always ready with a bit of humor to help a harried mother — actually, anyone — through the tough days. Case in point, from her blog for the *National Catholic Register*:

> Raising children brings so much joy, fulfillment, and meaning to life. It also brings guilt by the boatload. It is impossible to raise another human being without routinely screwing up in monumental ways — and that's when you're trying.

Spiritually mindful parents will recognize that wallowing under a load of crushing guilt is actually a subtle form of pride: By dwelling on our failures, we are making too much of ourselves, and too little of the redemptive power of grace, which can be accessed through daily acts of hope and trust in God and in Mary as the true mother of our children.

So that's for the holy types. For the rest of us, here is a handy cheat sheet....

THE OFFENSE:
It's the feast of St. Francis, and the kids are all giggling their way through Mass. You realize that they have been singing "Make Me a Panel of Your Cheese," which they learned from you.

THE SOLUTION:
Gasp and whisper furiously, "WHERE did you learn that?" Then sit on them before they can answer. When you get home, make kitten-shaped pancakes to make up for sitting on them.

Anna Mitchell, news director for the *Son Rise Morning Show*, is not afraid to admit that the single life can be hard, but she maintains a wry sense of humor. Here are her thoughts from an email about expectations for singles' conferences:

I mean, really, do people go to Catholic singles' conferences to merely learn how to be holy single people? Why do we ignore the fact that some (if not most, maybe all?)

single people attending this conference are probably also scoping out the crowd? I mean seriously, what's the point of a singles group? Is it just to grow in holiness as a single person? NO — it's also to meet other singles and hopefully form a relationship. It's not a bad thing to want to meet more single people and expand your options. I'd think it might be a good selling point, actually. A Catholic singles' conference is better than a bar, right?

<hr />

Barbara R. Nicolosi, screenwriter and founder of Act One, an organization for aspiring screenwriters, tackles the issue of engaging the culture with clarity and wisdom. She consistently speaks with a directness designed to get Christians to sit up, think, and act. Here's an excerpt from an interview with her on the Catholics United for the Faith website:

> I was talking to my undergrads at a college in Los Angeles — Christian kids … and I mentioned the phrase "patron of the arts." One of the kids in the front row raised his hand and said, "And who's that?"
>
> And I realized, looking at these 18-year-olds, that they didn't know the phrase "patron of the arts." So I said to them: "Well, who do *you* think the patron of the arts is? Talk about it among yourselves and then tell me what you think." And so they came back five minutes later, and they had two things that they had decided. One was Hugh Hefner of *Playboy Magazine*, and the other one was the Bravo channel.

And when I said to them, "No — the patron of the arts is the Church," they looked at me and they were like, "*What* art, and *what* Church?"

———————◆◆◆◆◆———————

Rebecca Ryskind Teti has an impressive background, but her charming biography that accompanies her posts for *Faith and Family* magazine captures her spirit perfectly:

Rebecca Teti is married to Dennis and has four children (three boys, one girl) who — like yours, no doubt — are pious and kind, gorgeous, and can spin flax into gold. A Washington, D.C., native, she converted to Catholicism while an undergrad at the U. Dallas, where she double-majored in political philosophy and drama. She holds an MA in political theory from Catholic University.... Rebecca now writes from home, with special interest in marriage and family issues, whatever the pope is doing, retrieving Lego bricks from underfoot, and homemade pie.

———————◆◆◆◆◆———————

Elizabeth Duffy blogs at bettyduffy.blogspot.com and tackles the minefield topic of sex in this book. She reveals her self-deprecating sense of humor in this blog post:

I used to see a priest for regular spiritual guidance, and one month, I started to unload about all the ways I felt my husband had slighted me. And the priest looked at me with a straight face, nodded his head, and said, "Boys are stupid." It was the point I was trying to make, so I went on, about how a girlfriend of mine said I should just tell him. . . .

The priest interrupted me, "Girls talk too much."

Only then did I realize that he wasn't commiserating with me.

Karen Edmisten, blogger and author, has a knack for getting to the heart of the matter when it comes to spirituality and the choices we face. She brought that sensibility to her testimony in the book *Atheist to Catholic: 11 Stories of Conversion*. This observation from that book captures the ongoing temptation we all face as we all struggle to fully surrender to God:

> I did wonder if a little Christianity might help — an idea here, a practice there, maybe some fasting. I could be kind to my neighbor, a little less snarky.

But I didn't want the whole package.

Now that you've met them, I hope you have some sense of why I was so eager to collaborate with these writers. They're funny, they're honest — and they're troupers, these women, because this process was not without its share of bumps along the way. But there was laughter and joy, too. In the end it was an adventure of the best kind.

Within the pages of this book you will find truth — not only the truth of these women's experiences, but also the truth as revealed by God through his Church. I hope it leaves you feeling encouraged and a little less alone. We're all in this together, and together we will prevail.

CHAPTER 1

How I Fell Out of My Minivan and Found Myself

Jennifer Fulwiler

The ladies at church seemed startled when I climbed out of the window of my minivan.

When the driver's-side door handle broke the week before, I decided to avoid the overwhelming task of getting it fixed by learning to live without a functioning car door. I was too tall to scoot over the seat and out the passenger side, but I grew up watching *The Dukes of Hazzard* and knew that entering and exiting vehicles through windows was a perfectly viable option. In fact, people wouldn't even realize that anything was wrong! They'd be so impressed with my smooth moves that they'd just think I was too awesome to open the door.

I quickly learned that the upper-body-strength to lower-body-weight ratio of the lean, male, twenty-something actors who starred in *The Dukes of Hazzard* is quite different from that of a thirty-four-year-old mother with a penchant for cookies-and-cream ice cream. Also, that the window of a minivan is about two feet higher off the ground than that of the sporty vehicle featured in the TV show.

Unfortunately, one of my first experiences with these realities occurred in front of my acquaintances from church.

A lady named Teresa, whom I knew through mutual friends, walked over to say hello. I tried to wave — this was mid-exit — but my foot got stuck in the steering wheel, and I lost my balance. I tumbled out the window, letting some profanity slip as I grasped for something to break my fall. Teresa glanced nervously at her children, probably not sure whether to assist me or flee while she had the chance.

I stood up, brushed myself off, and proceeded to make small talk. Assuming that she was also there to drop off her children at the parish Mothers' Day Out program, I made a little joke in reference to the increasingly ominous noises coming from inside my car. "If only we could drop them off by catapult, right?"

"We homeschool," she explained with a smile, nodding toward the three smartly dressed children standing politely beside her. "We're just here for daily Mass."

I glanced at my children in the car in time to see a baby doll fly through the air. My two-year-old was chewing on a shoe. I excused myself to haul the avalanche of kids and backpacks out of the minivan, and Teresa said goodbye and walked with her children toward the chapel.

Am I Doing Something Wrong Here?

After I dropped the kids off, I lumbered back through the window and sat in the driver's seat for a moment. This sort of thing happened all the time. I'd joyfully converted to Catholicism four years before, but I felt like I'd never quite found my footing. Intellectually, I had it down — I'd read enough books that I could *think* like a Catholic — but I seemed to be failing at *being* a Catholic.

While other women enjoyed joining prayer groups and running ministries, I was so introverted that my spiritual director once joked that I should have been a desert hermit. When I did attempt to socialize at the parish, such as my morning exchange with Teresa, it only added credence to that theory.

I had a specific idea of what the authentic Catholic woman was like: She was the picture of joy and grace every time she went to Mass and always had an emotionally powerful experience upon receiving the Eucharist; she kept her home tidy, and she joyfully crafted elaborate celebrations for each liturgical season.

And then there is me. I have five young children spaced so closely together that fellow Catholics, when they first meet my husband and me, often ask, "Would you like to borrow our Natural Family Planning book?" Mass is usually more of an exercise in survival than something I enjoy on an emotional level. My house is not exactly neat, and my biggest success with celebrating the liturgical year had been buying a package of purple napkins one Advent.

There in the driver's seat of my van, I noticed scuff marks on my blue jeans from my encounter with the parking lot pavement, and I thought of how lovely my friend Teresa had looked with her colorful, flowing skirt and her neatly pressed blouse. Comparing myself with her and all the others I perceived to be true Catholic women, I sank a little lower into the seat. I wanted to say a pious prayer beseeching the Lord for assistance, but all I could come up with was:

Lord, I am failing at this whole Catholic womanhood thing!

I started the car, pulled out of the parking lot, and prayed all the way home. I even spent a few moments in silence when I got back to the house instead of rushing over to my laptop as was my habit. I begged God to show me what it meant for someone like me to be authentically Catholic.

The Search for the Modern Mary

Shortly after saying that prayer, I had an idea: I should search for a role model, specifically for an image of what the Blessed Mother would look like if she lived in the twenty-first century. Having a visual would give me something to cling to when I strayed off course; it would provide a clear goal as I transformed myself into a real Catholic woman.

I picked up a magazine from the stack next to the couch and flipped through it, evaluating one depiction of a modern woman after another. I was fairly certain that God had given me this idea, so I figured he must have some exciting solution in store. I couldn't wait to find my image.

Nothing struck me in the magazine, so I turned to the Internet and browsed everything from oil paintings to ads to clip art, all the while asking, "What would Mary look like if she lived here and now?" Would her hair be short or long? Would she wear blouses or T-shirts? Would her face reveal an expression of unbridled joy or serious contemplation? No answer came. I kept looking.

"How Gloriously Different All the Saints"

I didn't find an image that day, or the day after. In fact, my search stretched on for weeks. Meanwhile, I kept thinking about the concept of true Catholic womanhood. I took a closer look at the lives of female saints and kept my ears perked for any Church teaching on the subject. What I discovered surprised me.

From the beginning of my conversion, I'd been aware of the call to die to self and become like Christ. In the Gospel of John we read that, "He must increase, but I must decrease (3:30, RSV)." In his letter to the Galatians, Paul says that he no longer lives, but Christ lives in him (Gal. 2:20). In *Lumen Gentium* (the Second Vatican Council's Dogmatic Constitution on the Church), we read, "All the members [of the Body of Christ] ought to be molded in the likeness of Him, until Christ be formed in them."[1]

Here's how I understood these teachings: Becoming like Christ meant becoming unlike yourself. I had a rigid idea of what a devout person looked like and assumed that all holy people were basically carbon copies of one another. But that's not what I found when I looked more closely at the lives of the saints.

For example, I discovered that while many were naturally at ease in social situations, such as the gifted administrator and teacher St. Frances Cabrini, or St. Elizabeth Ann Seton, who captivated everyone with her charm, some were not. St. Frances of Rome was so introverted that she suffered a serious breakdown after the banquets and parties that accompanied her marriage!

And when it came to marriage, some saints were happily married, such as St. Margaret of Scotland; some had difficult marriages, such as St. Monica; some were separated from their husbands, such as St. Radegunde and St. Etheldreda; and some, like St. Helena, were divorced.

Of course, all the female servants of God throughout the ages lived in quiet, orderly environments that were perfectly conducive to prayer, right? This was impossible for women like me with large families. But then I encountered St. Jeanne de Lestonnac, who ran her estate by herself after her husband died, in addition to raising five children. St. Margaret of Scotland and St. Bridget of Sweden each had eight children, and St. Joaquina Vedruna had nine.

By now my stereotypical thinking was in full retreat, including the notion that the saints were happy all the time. I learned that St. Catherine of Genoa battled severe depression for years, and I was as surprised as the rest of the world when it became clear that Bl. Mother Teresa heroically endured fifty years of the "dark night of the soul." Even super-saint Thérèse of Lisieux went through a final period of intense interior darkness before her death.

C.S. Lewis once observed, "How monotonously alike all the great tyrants and conquerors have been: how gloriously different all the saints."[2] I had to agree. When I took a fresh look at real Christian holiness, this is what I found: Diversity. Uniqueness. People of all different temperaments and lifestyles, with a wide array of personal strengths and weaknesses.

Lumen Gentium specifically praised the different forms that holiness can take, noting that the Holy Spirit "distributes special graces among the faithful of every rank," and that "by these gifts He makes them fit and ready to undertake the various tasks ... which contribute toward the renewal and building up of the Church." The Church is praised for having a "wonderful diversity," where "each individual part contributes through its special gifts to the good of the other parts and of the whole Church."[3]

In other words, there is not a one-size-fits-all template for being a good Catholic. I didn't have to ape women like my friend Teresa in order to live my faith to the fullest.

It was time to take another look at what Catholic womanhood might mean for *me*.

Discovering Your Unique Type of Holiness

I threw myself into this quest, reading everything I could find on the subject and consulting confessors and a spiritual director. This is what I learned: To uncover your unique brand of holiness, you have to sift your God-given quirks and talents from your sins. So, for example, I shouldn't feel bad about the fact that I'm the type of person who sometimes ends up stumbling out of the car window at church. God gave me a brain that drifts toward quirky ideas. Instead of bemoaning that, I should ask how I can use that unique characteristic to do his work. But my occasional use of profanity and tendency to complain about everything? Those should go.

I began to carefully discern the areas where sins and quirks collide, such as my relationship with housekeeping. I'd embraced the fact that with my scatterbrained nature, I'm not a naturally gifted homemaker. My house is never going to look like something out of a lifestyle magazine. But it was also clear that sometimes the sin of sloth was at work when I neglected to keep my living space clean. Taking this to confession, I received the grace to begin to reject my slothful behavior while still accepting my God-given nature.

As the sifting process went on, something surprising happened: I was unearthing my real self. Before my conversion, I had confused certain sinful tendencies with inherent personality traits. To be truly myself, I thought, was to be cynical, short-tempered, and lazy. *That's just who I am,* I rationalized. But I've come to understand that to be a saint is, among other things, to be wholly yourself. The more time I spent asking God to show me what it meant for me to be a good Catholic, the more I realized that he was showing me what it meant to be *me.*

This brought a peace with who I am and a comfort in my own skin that I'd never known was possible. The inner transformation created a ripple effect in almost every area of my life.

Once I realized that I didn't have to be like my seemingly perfect friend Teresa, I was able to relax and get to know women like her on a deeper level, drawing inspiration from them rather than comparing myself to them. Sure enough, I found that they often had struggles in areas I didn't. Now that I wasn't so worried about "failing" according to some preconceived notion of what it means to observe the Church year, I even stepped up my celebrations of the liturgical seasons, buying purple napkins *and* a wreath one Advent — though I usually forgot to light the candles.

Sister Bridget Haase once counseled listeners of her radio show to "sparkle with self-forgetfulness." In order to show others the love of Christ, she explained, you have to think of others more than you think of yourself. Ironically, my insecurity about how to be a Catholic woman the "right" way had led me to focus almost exclusively on myself. When I socialized, I was always more concerned about whether I was saying something inappropriate or un-Catholic than I was about the well-being of the people around me. It was only when I learned to accept myself that I could forget myself; and it was only then that I could show others the love of Christ.

The Answer to the Prayer

In the midst of these discoveries, my effort to find an image of the modern Mary had shifted to the back burner. I suspected that the notion to pray for such a guide was not inspired by the Holy Spirit after all, but was just another of my zany ideas.

Then one afternoon, as I walked through my living room, my mind abuzz with a hundred other thoughts, something caught my eye. I stopped in my tracks. It was one of those rare moments when the presence of the Holy Spirit is palpable, as if a breeze had swept through the room. I stared in bewildered surprise at — a mirror.

More precisely, at my reflection in a mirror. A chill went through me. My prayer had been answered: Here was my image of the modern Mary.

When she lived on earth, the Mother of God was probably not tall with pale skin and blue eyes, but I sensed God telling me, as I stared at my reflection, *This is what a holy woman can look like.* If I wanted an image that captured true Catholic womanhood for me, I need look no further than the image of the woman in the mirror.

I stared for a moment at the familiar visage of the tired mom in jeans and a T-shirt. When I imagined her as the picture of perfect holiness, everything changed. I stood a little straighter. I smiled, and the weary expression on my face faded away. I saw my great potential and forgot about my faults.

At that moment, all the lessons I'd been learning sunk in on a visceral level. I took another glance at that woman, the person I'd thought of as outside the iron mold of what a Catholic woman looked like. Not only could she be a good Catholic woman, I realized, but God could use even her to change the world.

Reject Your Sins, Love Your Quirks, and Go Change the World

Though some of us have been slow to catch on, the Church has always celebrated the many faces of true Catholic femininity. At the triumphant end of the apostolic letter *Mulieris Dignitatem*, Pope John Paul II proclaims:

> *The Church gives thanks for each and every woman*: for mothers, for sisters, for wives; for women consecrated to God in virginity; for women dedicated to the many human beings who await the gratuitous love of another person; for women who watch over the human persons in the family, which is the fundamental sign of the human community; for women who work professionally, and who at times are burdened by a great social responsibility; for *"perfect"* women and for "weak" women — for all women as they have come forth from the heart of God in all the beauty and richness of their femininity. ...

The Church gives thanks *for all the manifestations of the feminine "genius"* which have appeared in the course of history ... she gives thanks for all *the fruits of feminine holiness.*[4]

Notice how Bl. John Paul II emphasizes the rich *variety* that exists among great Catholic women. From papal documents to the lives of the saints, the Church sends us the message over and over again: There is no one right path to authentic Catholic womanhood. God has a special plan for your unique gifts and talents.

St. Catherine of Siena famously stated, "Be who God meant you to be, and you will set the world on fire." We tend to focus on the second, more dramatic part of the statement, but the first is just as important: *Be who God meant you to be.* Embrace the one-of-a-kind brand of holiness that God has chosen for you. Reject your sins, but love your quirks. And the next time you look in a mirror, remember that you're looking at a woman who can set the world on fire.

❧❧

Embrace the one-of-a-kind brand of holiness that God has chosen for you. Reject your sins, but love your quirks.

❧❧

QUESTIONS FOR REFLECTION

1. In what area of your life do your sins and quirks collide? How can you accept your God-given temperament in this area without rationalizing your sins?

2. Do you tend to compare yourself to other women? If so, what kind of characteristics do they have? Are these traits that you should work on adopting as well, or should you accept that that's not how God made you?

3. What is an aspect of your personality that you may have considered a fault, but is actually a strength? How might God use that to bless others through you?

4. What saint has challenged your ideas about what holy people are like? What did he or she do that surprised you?

5. Take a moment to imagine the Blessed Mother looking just like you and having your exact life. What is the number one thing she'd do differently on a daily basis?

6. Imagine the Blessed Mother with your life again. This time, consider what she would do the same as you do. Think about some occasions when you've shown the love of Mary to the people around you. How did that effort influence a situation or help someone?

Jennifer Fulwiler is a writer, speaker, and atheist-to-Catholic convert who blogs at ConversionDiary.com. She lives in Austin, Texas, with her husband and five young children and now drives a minivan with a functioning door.

CHAPTER 2

Style:
Balance, Beauty,
and You

Hallie Lord

It's not an altogether pleasant experience to divulge that what first led you to the Church was a person's sense of style. I mean, how shallow do you have to be? Who doesn't have a story of how G.K. Chesterton escorted them home to Rome with his insight and wit? Or of how Teresa of Avila brought them to their knees with her fearless exhortations?

I don't.

Do you know who first compelled me to knock so that the door could be opened? A rockabilly girl with the cutest dress I ever did see.

Perhaps it sounds superficial, but God works in mysterious ways, does he not? And so he did by bringing me face to face with a girl who looked an awful lot like me, but spoke beautiful words whose meanings were a mystery — words such as *conversion, devotion,* and *faith.* And words more jarring still: *Christ,* and *Eucharist,* and *sin,* and *redemption.* Even stranger, these words rolled off her tongue free of self-consciousness and unrestrained by shame.

It was 1999. I was twenty years old and just starting to wrestle with that feeling of anxiety that many converts experience. I couldn't put my finger on exactly what was wrong, but I knew — with a certainty that I couldn't shake — that something was amiss. Only later would I be able to identify this feeling as the feeling that comes with a soul displaced. My soul was longing for home, begging me to find true north, but it wasn't until that girl with the Bettie Page bangs and the Mary Jane heels opened her mouth that it began to dawn on me that perhaps I was lost. And that just maybe, I could be found.

As it often is with conversion, I didn't immediately run to the nearest church and fall prostrate in front of a crucifix. In fact, I would spend two years turning toward Rome and then away and then back again before I bowed and received into my body that same transfigured God that the humble rockabilly girl had spoken of so eloquently. She never left my side, though. Her image stayed with me through those two tumultuous years and comforted me along the way.

Conversion comes without the gnashing of teeth to very few. Even after the truth is mercifully revealed to us converts, we still must battle against that part of ourselves that holds on so desperately to the things we held dear in our former life:

I don't want to give up my vision of the future, which I so painstakingly crafted over the last however-many years.

I don't want to give up sexual autonomy and selfishness, materialism and control.

I don't want to give up my identity to become more like him.

But, of course, giving up our identity isn't what he asks of us, is it? Yes, we are called to constant conversion. Yes, we are called to become more Christ-like. But we are not called to jettison our personalities and passions.

Through the expression of her individuality, the girl I saw on that day so long ago showed me that I could become a Christian and still be me. Indeed, I would have to surrender many worldly things and sacrifice much, but I could still be me. My view of the world and my understanding of my place in it might radically change, but I could still be me.

I needed to know that. I needed to see that to be open to conversion.

So, yes, it was that image that first piqued this convert's interest. There's still a part of me that is mildly embarrassed about that fact, but there's another part of me that is humbled by it — humbled because it shows that God meets us right where we are. And that is an awesome thing indeed.

Giving up our identity isn't what Christ asks of us, is it? Yes, we are called to constant conversion, but we are not called to jettison our personalities and passions.

Meeting Modesty

It didn't take long to realize that a few adjustments to my fashion sense were in order once I became Catholic. No longer did I feel right about wearing vintage slips and stilettos (and *only* vintage slips and stilettos) when I went out on the town. And streaking down a beach at midnight with nary a stitch on? That was definitely going to have to go. For the first time in my life, that loaded "M" word (you know the one: *modesty*) was on my radar, and it was proving a tough thing to navigate.

There are no hard and fast rules when it comes to modesty. How modesty will be integrated into each woman's life is left up to her individual conscience. That's not to say that great saints haven't advised us on the issue, or that the *magisterium* has nothing to say about it, but, ultimately, the details are left for us to sort out.

This was not great news for a young girl whose conscience, when it came to issues of sexuality, had never been properly formed. I could surmise that I should probably make some effort to obscure my cleavage, but what about my collarbone? I supposed that hot pants were a no-no, but were bare knees okay?

Desperately wanting to be virtuous after years of embracing sexual immorality, I went to an extreme. I turned my back on the world of fashion and chose shapeless, long dresses that tickled my ankles. I locked my makeup away and embraced simpler (read: unattractive) hairstyles. After all, I concluded, modesty didn't simply mean not exposing the most intimate parts of my body, but also suggested that I not draw undue attention to myself, right?

Absolutely. And I failed miserably.

What people saw was not a woman who was at peace with her appearance, but a woman who was ill at ease, self-conscious, and ashamed. In retrospect, I think I was trying to do penance for past sins, but trying to become invisible did not yield good fruit.

I was unintentionally sending a message to my husband that now that we were married, I no longer cared about catching his eye. I was showing those who had watched my journey home to Rome with skepticism that conversion entails losing your individuality. (Ironically, I'd temporarily forgotten that stylish girl who first made me glance at Christianity.) And, because I was so self-conscious and uncomfortable, I was sending a message to the world that I didn't want to be approached or befriended.

While it's clear now that my brief detour in pursuit of invisibility was not my ultimate destination, it did teach me a three important things:

- Modesty is compatible with stylishness. There's a pervasive misconception that in order to dress modestly, you must consign yourself to a life of wearing potato sacks. Nothing could be further from the truth. Embracing modesty does not mean hiding your feminine figure; it simply means hiding the intimate details of your body from the world at large.

- Dressing well increases confidence. When I look my best, I feel my best. It's as simple as that. Who doesn't have an extra spring in her step on the days that she wears her favorite outfit? This added *joie de vivre* allows us to face our challenges with more joy, less fear, and greater success.

- Though the catwalks of New York are not known for their modesty, there's a level of artistry there that I can appreciate. As someone who loves fashion, it can be tempting to jettison my sense of morality to embrace the latest looks. Only when I marry style with modesty do I feel a sense of peace, though. Only then am I in tune with God's will.

For me, Edith Head captured it best when she said: "A dress should be tight enough to show you're a woman and loose enough to prove you're a lady."

Indeed.

The Power of Transformation

Anyone with a cable connection knows how wildly popular makeover shows have become. They're as close to a sure thing as a television producer can get.

The curtain opens to reveal a bewildered woman who appears to have been plucked from the forest and seems confused by the term "hairbrush." A mere thirty minutes later she's channeling Norma Desmond and is ready for her close-up. It's a lot of smoke and mirrors, yes, but we keep coming back for more.

Why is this?

The easy and obvious conclusion is that we live in a shallow society obsessed with the physical. Well, that's certainly true. I think there's more, though.

The reason we gasp with amazement when we see the newly made-over person unveiled is because we recognize that something big has happened here — something that goes beyond a new haircut or a fresh coat of lipstick. The person now gives off entirely different energy. She is the same person she always was, but her new physical appearance brings forth elements of herself that were hidden before — elements that have the potential to effect change not only in her own life, but in the lives of all with whom she comes into contact. That's no small thing, and we know it.

Wrestling with Vanity

One question that rightly gets raised when the topic of personal appearance is broached: How do we handle the vanity issue? After all, as Catholics, aren't we supposed to renounce worldly goods? Die to self? Embrace humility?

How does a woman do this when she must rise each day and dress herself in clothes suitable for her many activities? Is she truly dying to self when she shops for shoes that please her husband, but in the end please her even more? And when she experiences that familiar sensation of womanly delight that comes from appreciating her new haircut, can she truly say that she's conquered vanity?

I think that we ought to consider motive. Of course, motives are rarely perfectly pure, but as the late great Chesterton once said, "Anything worth doing is worth doing badly."

What constitutes a thing "worth doing" in the life of a lay Catholic woman? Well, for this woman, I want my husband to know that even after a decade of marriage I still like to catch his eye. I want my children to know that my vocation has value and is worthy of respect (certainly not the message I send when I wear sweat pants or pajamas all day long). And I want the world to see that I am thriving as a twenty-first-century Catholic woman.

All of those things require that I put some energy into my appearance. How do we settle into that comfortable middle between letting ourselves go and becoming preoccupied with physical appearance? I think we can begin by routinely asking ourselves this question: Why do we do the things we do?

For instance ...

Why do I set aside time for myself to exercise? Is it because I want others to find me attractive and am trying to avoid my to-do list? Or is it because I want to have enough energy to play with my children, feather my nest, contribute to society, and nurture my marriage?

Why do I buy new, flattering clothes, style my hair, and wear a touch of makeup? Is it to nurture the sexual-love aspect of my marriage? Is it to demonstrate to the world that I am approachable and relatable? Or is strictly for my own satisfaction?

Well, who are we kidding? All but the holiest among us will probably reply, "All of the above." And that's okay. Most of us are going to struggle from time to time — and to differing degrees — with vanity, materialism, and mixed motives. I refuse to just give up, though. As long as the motives are mixed — and not solely selfish — I say carry on. We're all works in progress.

A friend recently shared a piece of advice her spiritual director gave her. She had been feeling frustrated by the fact that vanity kept encroaching on her efforts to get in shape. Her primary motivation was honorable — she simply wanted to put her best foot forward — but she was concerned about the fact that it seemed to go hand in hand with this vice.

Her spiritual director gently pointed out that it was a form of pride for her to find this so surprising. She suggested that a saint would react by laughing at herself, accepting that (of course) a weak person like her would be tempted by this sin, and simply cling to the sacrament of confession. It took a lot of weight off of my friend's shoulders to recognize that she's susceptible to this sin, that this temptation isn't likely to leave her soon, and that she can turn to the sacraments for grace in handling this tendency.

We live in a difficult time. We're surrounded by a society in which vanity has become a virtue and the understanding of virtue confused. Women are constantly tempted in this area. Even as we fight the good fight, it is imperative that we are patient with and merciful toward ourselves.

Finding Balance

Let's face it: There are seasons of life when all the vanity (or desire to be an effective witness) in the world couldn't compel you — or give you the energy required — to pull a hairbrush through your hair or apply a bit of lipstick! Some seasons are just like that. Some seasons are survival seasons.

Whether you're a single woman trying to balance career, family responsibilities, and a busy social calendar, or a married woman building a family and nurturing a marriage, we all have those days, weeks, and even years when making sure we eat the bare minimum to get by and occasionally take a shower is about all of the self-care we can manage.

Seasons like these demand balance.

In the beginning, when these times were upon me, I went to the perfectionist extreme. It didn't matter that I'd only had three hours of interrupted sleep the night before, hadn't taken a shower in days and subsisted on a diet of strong coffee and Peanut M&Ms. I was determined that no woman on the face of the earth would do a better June Cleaver impression — high heels and all — than I. Guess where that left me?

Completely burned out.

So I gave up. I wore yoga pants all day, every day; stuck my makeup in the back of the closet; and jettisoned my exercise habit. I gained weight, looked terrible, and felt even worse. My self-esteem plummeted; and as a result of that, my marriage suffered. This extreme caused me much more grief than my perfectionist phase ever had. In many ways, I'm still pulling out of it.

I think I understand balance better these days. It's a constant struggle as seasons of plenty and of want come and go, as hormones fluctuate, and as life throws new challenges in my direction. But this much I know: We women have got to find a way to be merciful toward ourselves without completely throwing in the towel; to surrender to the hard times while still fighting for our ideals; and to remain open to God's grace while accepting that sometimes that grace isn't going to look and feel how we might hope.

So how do we do this? With a whole lot of prayer and a few good habits. For my part, I've discovered one simple rule that helps me more than anything else in accomplishing this goal: Each day I do one small thing for myself.

When I stumble out of bed bleary-eyed from a night of little sleep and burdened by the weight of the world, the thought of showering, finding a cute outfit, applying make-up, and blow-drying my hair (and this all before the children wake up) is enough to send me straight back to bed. It's just too much. So I don't even try. I've learned the hard way that it's nothing more than a recipe for disappointment and defeat. But I refuse to throw in the towel and give up entirely, either.

On the hard days, I may only have time to apply a touch of sweet-smelling moisturizer or to slip into my favorite dress. On less difficult days, I savor leisurely exercise and long baths. I never fail to be surprised by what a difference these small acts of loving discipline can make.

It's not just that I feel a little prettier or healthier when I do these things (though I do, and that lifts my spirits immensely). It's somehow bigger than that. It sends a signal that my being well is important and is worth fighting for. That can be an easy thing to forget when you're caught up in the busyness of day-to-day life; but if we aim to thrive, it's not something we can afford to forget.

Taking Care of You

In short, as the saying goes, you need to put on your own oxygen mask first. I realize it might sound trite, but it's a message worth meditating on.

I know it feels funny. We women, by our very nature, are born nurturers. Most of us are more comfortable in self-sacrifice mode than we are tending to our own needs. It can feel uncomfortable to press the pause button to take care of yourself when you could be doing something to make the world a better place. Ultimately, though, we'll be more effective at bettering our world if we take some time to nurture ourselves first. To give of yourself, you have to have something to give.

I realize that in today's culture some women take this thinking to an extreme, which is regrettable and certainly not what I'm suggesting. We don't have too many "ladies who lunch" in the ranks of the modern female Church Militant, though. I see much more radical self-giving than I do self-indulgence — which is wonderful — but if we're going to keep that going, we must find ways to avoid burnout.

Every woman's physical needs are going to manifest themselves differently. At a bare minimum, though, we ought to be striving for four things: healthy eating, regular exercise, adequate rest, and occasional peaceful pampering.

Crazy, right?

Maybe, but also essential. I know what you're thinking. In an ideal world, you'd be all over this proposed model. But in real life? Impossible. If that's the case, I'd say that a little creative restructuring might be in order. I firmly believe that not having time for basic personal care is a symptom of a problem, not something to embrace.

If you wake up in the morning and open your closet only to find that you have nothing that fits but pajamas and sweatpants, that's a problem.

If you find yourself never wanting to socialize because you feel badly about your appearance, that's a problem.

If you avoid intimacy with your husband because you feel unattractive, that's a problem.

If you are constantly tired because you never have time to exercise, rest, or spend time alone, that, too, is a problem.

It may seem that these things should be pretty far down the list of life's priorities, but I submit to you that they are essential. The way a woman feels about and perceives herself physically will have ramifications that extend to the rest of her life. It will affect the way she interacts with her children, her husband, and her community. It will affect her very relationship with God.

If the above list sounds familiar, I implore you to sit down, take a hard look at your life, and make some changes. In the not-too-distant future, something is going to give; and for the sake of yourself, your husband, and your children, it should not be you.

Maybe you're a person for whom it is hard to say "no." Practice.

Maybe you find yourself surrounded by people who demand too much from you. Set boundaries.

Maybe you don't know why your life feels chaotic and don't know how to begin to fix it. Pray. God will give you the solution you seek.

If you're tempted to shy away from tending to your needs, remember that, ultimately, it's not just for you; it's for every person you come into contact with. A woman who feels confident, happy, and self-assured is a woman who will spread light wherever she goes.

That woman will transform the world.

QUESTIONS FOR REFLECTION

1. Are you comfortable embracing and expressing your individuality? If not, why not? If so, how has this strong sense of identity benefited you in your life?

2. Do you struggle with modesty? Do you find yourself going to one extreme or another? What things could you do to make peace with this issue?

3. Do you think that physical appearance can be used for the purpose of evangelization? Why or why not?

4. Do you feel guilty when you take time to nurture yourself and tend to your needs? If so, where do these feelings of guilt come from? Your spouse? Other family members? Friends? Can you think of a way to charitably express your needs to those who are not currently supportive?

5. What is one small thing you can do to lift your spirits each day?

6. Which area of your life do you feel is most out of balance? What would it take to restore balance in this area?

Hallie Lord is a wife, mother of five, and convert to Catholicism. When not corralling small children or flirting with her husband, she is a freelance writer and style consultant. You can find her online at BettyBeguiles.com.

CHAPTER 3

God and Godiva

Karen Edmisten

Who is this contemporary Catholic woman of whom we speak? Let's take a quick inventory, shall we?

We work in the home and in the public square. We go to Mass every single Sunday (sometimes more), eat bread that we call God and sip wine we call Blood. We care about what that anciently-robed guy in Rome says, and we spill our sins to another human being. We mate for life. We shun artificial birth control. Let's face it — we're, umm, *different.* We're proudly pope-loving, sterilization-eschewing, Eucharist-adoring, confession-going, twenty-first-century Catholic specimens of femininity who buck societal norms and balk at contemporary expectations. Yeah, we're the face of the new rebellion.

Scary, aren't we?

I used to be a different kind of scary. As a young woman I also battled societal norms: I didn't want marriage or babies; I was content with cohabitation. I embraced the perceived control of contraception, and I marched to maintain abortion-on-demand. I rebelled against traditional morality; and if the world found such radical ideas scary, I found the world sorely in need of brains and tolerance.

Now that society has grown so enlightened, I'm the scary one again, because just when I thought I'd come back to the fold, I found that embracing old norms made me, once more, the outsider. (It seems rebellious now to *not* get a tattoo.)

Funny that I've always been attracted to the countercultural. I used to dodge the religious fanatics, and now I'm the Jesus freak and defender of all things Crazy-Catholic. Having sex without birth control? But what if I get pregnant in my forties? (I did.) Staying married forever and ever? But what if we hit a rocky road and become unhappy? (We did. We were. We went through some torture to work it out, and we're in love again.) Buying into all that stuff about bread and wine being Body and Blood? (Hook, line, and sinker.) The result of my transformation is a life that is more stable, content, and full of love and freedom than anything I knew in the days when I thought I was unencumbered.

The challenge of holding on to our faith in a postmodern society is figuring out how to be in the world — a light, we hope, by the grace of God — but not of it. "I even believe," said Edith Stein, now known as St. Teresa Benedicta of the Cross, "that the deeper one is drawn into God, the more one must 'go out of oneself'; that is, one must go to the world in order to carry the divine life into it."[5]

How do I do that? How do you? How do we help each other do it?

The temptations to absorb the world into our marrow are many; they vary for each of us. But no matter what the temptations, the solution to conquering them is the same: grace and prayer, the sacraments, accountability, spiritual support from others, and ongoing discernment to keep our relationship with God flourishing. I'll not deny, however, that coffee, Nutella, and Cabernet Sauvignon have their place.

What to Do: Prayer and the Sacraments

We know what it is. We know we need to do it. And we agonize over fitting it in. But without prayer, we haven't got a prayer. We know that a marriage can't survive without intimacy and that a friendship can't thrive when there's no conversation. We've *got* to talk to God, plain and simple. And we need to listen, too. I start with the simple premise that I will talk to him every day. I can't guarantee I'll always be a sparkling conversationalist, but I promise to show up. Here are a few of the things I've learned over the years.

A Morning Offering

Whether short and sweet (such as the one I do with my youngest daughter: "Dear Lord, I give you this day, all that I think, all that I say, all that I do, I give to you!") or long and traditional (the one I do in the shower — more on that later), offer your entire day and its activity to God. This is not cheating, but it has the delicious feel of a shortcut that really works and gets you to your destination in record time.

A Bedtime Examination of Conscience

Before falling asleep, do a quick mental review of your day: "Did I act like a fallen human today? (Sigh.) Yes, I did. *Again*!

Doh, I keep doing that! Okay, God, sorry for _____" and you may fill in the blank accordingly. If the blank is too long or contains too many scary symbols (#&*!##%&!), you may want to consider getting to confession.

Pray in Rhythm with the Church

Don't panic — this rhythm doesn't involve a tambourine or any embarrassing public dancing. I'm referring to the Liturgy of the Hours, also known as the breviary or the Divine Office.

These "prayers of the Church" are intoned daily by all ordained and vowed religious. If you've heard of Morning Prayer, Evening Prayer, and so on, you're halfway there. Once upon a time, you had to spend an unholy amount of money on a set of four thick books that boasted so many ribbons I considered using some of them in my daughter's hair. But now it's easy. Everything is online or on your phone. Try iBreviary or DivineOffice.org to get started. I don't pray all the hours — I'd never have time to make dinner — but the benefits of a sprinkling are myriad. Adding just a couple of Psalms to your day or some of the readings from the Church Fathers is an effortless way to stay in touch with God's word and his Church.

Getting to Mass

The greatest prayer of the Church is the Holy Sacrifice of the Mass. Is there anything you can do to pray it more often? One extra Mass a month? A week? Any commitment that works for you is worth the effort.

Getting to Confession

Are you a Dorothy Parker penitent? Parker, a writer, said of her profession, "Hate to write, love having written." I apply her aphorism to the Sacrament of Penance. Hate to go, love having gone. So I try not to ponder it. I just go. If I ponder, I will procrastinate and will undoubtedly find a closet to rearrange, a phone call to return, an email to write, or something to shop for. Don't think. *Just go.*

If you have any kind of problem with confession at your home parish, drive to another one. Jesus is in every single confessional.

Feed Somebody

Really. We Catholics are a sacramental bunch, embracing the stuff of earth and connecting it to heaven. It doesn't get more earthy than our need for daily bread. This stuff is all over Scripture — Jesus heals a little girl and immediately says, "Hey, get her some food." He rises from the dead, and while his apostles are still reeling from shock and joy, Jesus cuts to the chase, asking for a bite to eat.

My friend Kathy prays every time she cooks and bakes — she asks God to bless the food and those who will eat it. This is a much holier attitude than mine, which is generally, "Jesus told me to pick up my cross and follow him, so, *fine*, I'll cook dinner!"

Healing and food, feedings and love, the mundane and the sublime go hand in hand. So if you can't seem to pray, make somebody some pancakes.

Fully Embrace Your Vocation or Current State in Life

Whether you're single, married, or discerning a call to religious life, deliriously happy or a confused mess, offer it up to God. Give him every moment. Prayers and pleas muttered throughout the day (God loves intimate muttering, I'm sure of it) are a great way to stay in touch with him. Mutterings possibly heard at my house:

- "I hate to cook. But, okay — for you, Lord."

- "Really? *More* laundry? Why do my kids create laundry day after endless 100 percent cotton day? But, okay — for you, Lord."

- "A writing deadline! I'll never get it done on time!" morphs into, "Thank you, Lord, for the chance to do this work, but I'm gonna make a deal. I know I said I'd cook, but if I'm writing can we have frozen pizza tonight?"

Whether you're single, married, or discerning a call to religious life, deliriously happy or a confused mess, offer it up to God. Give him every moment.

Dance in the Kitchen

What kind of music makes you think of God? Play it. Right now. Bach? Bluegrass? Contemporary Christian?

Rock? Chant? Jazz? Sesame Street with your toddler? If it lifts you out of yourself, listen. And dance. And thank God for the raw and energizing power of music.

A Holy Hour

A lot of people shy away from one, fearing they can't commit. If your current schedule prohibits an hour of Adoration, consider a holy half-hour, or even a pretty-darn-holy fifteen minutes. Do you have time once a week, or biweekly, or once a month? On the way home from work, on an errand day, before grocery shopping, or after dropping kids at school, stop in church and bask in the presence of Jesus in the tabernacle now and then.

Pray like a Pirate

My spiritual director once mentioned the "A-R-R-R" method of prayer, and I immediately dubbed it pirate prayer. A-R-R-R means "Acknowledge, Relate, Receive, and Respond." Here's a quick walk through this helpful way to pray:

- **Acknowledge** what I'm *really* thinking and feeling, not what I wish I felt, or what I think God would have me feel. Admit the truth — no matter how irrational, unjustifiable, or unpleasant it is.

- **Relate**: Hand that truth over to God. Lay it at his feet. Give it to him, utterly and completely.

- ◆ **Receive**: What is God offering me in response? Is he calling me to forgiveness, action, grieving, healing? Be open. (This doesn't always come right away — be patient, too.)

- ◆ **Respond**: How will I put God's response into practice?

In reality, these steps don't always happen in convenient bullet form. "Acknowledge and Relate" may stretch out over weeks or months before I'm ready to move on, because I have to empty myself of self before I can receive anything from the Lord. But I also can't get stuck in Acknowledge and Relate. Reminding myself that it's a process is vital. Knowing that I'm only one or two steps into a course of action wards off despair and nurtures hope. Who knew pirates were so spiritually attuned?

Make Your Prayers Visible

My friend Johnna, a mother of eight, stations strategic visual reminders around her house to help her focus on her calling. "When I'm in the midst of chaos," she said, "which is our house most of the time, I need to *see* that I am not alone." The corporal works of mercy are labeled in various rooms of the house. A homemade sign exhorting, "Feed the hungry" is taped to a cupboard. "Give drink to the thirsty" is above the kitchen sink, and "Clothe the naked" graces the washing machine. The time-out chair beckons, "Visit the Imprisoned."

I share my friend's love of the visual. My family and I made a poster — Words to Live By — that hangs in our kitchen. We add quotes, ideas, Bible verses, and inspiring thoughts whenever they hit us. Beautiful, edifying art, Scripture posted on the fridge, and my Bavarian Madonna statue are a few of the other things that round out our visible prayers.

When to Do It (Or, We Are Experiencing Scheduling Difficulties)

Theoretically, the *when* of prayer is simpler than the *what*. We pick a time, and we commune with God, right? Eh, not so fast there, missy. In my experience, life rarely goes as planned. We all keep waiting for that golden, magical moment when life will settle down, and everything will shimmer and waft dreamily into place. *Listen to me very carefully*: Life doesn't settle down. Not on this side of heaven. Still, there are a few things we can do to help our messy, unshimmery lives run a little more smoothly.

Your Planner, Your Friend

Whether you use a smartphone, a day planner, or sticky notes slapped on the fridge, schedule stuff. Schedules make things happen. Relying on "Someday...." does not. Want to commit to a daily Mass once a month? Pick a day and get it on the calendar. Commitments − Priorities. Vague thoughts such as, "Wouldn't it be lovely to get to Mass more often?" don't grow teeth and bones. Put stuff on the calendar.

The same goes for confession. Put it in writing. Save the date: "Saturday, the 8th: Wail. Gnash teeth. Confess. Feel flood of grace and relief. Eat some Godiva."

Double Duty: Pair Activities with Prayers

When my second daughter was born, I thought I'd never pray again. Or shower. Eventually I combined the two. When she was a baby, my ablutions weren't always regular or solitary, but when I could swing it, a hot shower turned out to be a spiffy place to pray. It still is. The routine has evolved into this: my daily offering, then prayers for the kids. Next, I pray for conversions — my own ongoing, so sorely needed, and others — and specific intentions. Finally, I ask the intercession of the saints, including the babies we've lost through miscarriage.

This prayer-activity combo works for so many tasks, and it's ridiculously easy. You can pray for your family when you wash dishes; pray for long-distance friends during the morning commute; pray for the poor and homeless while throwing in a load of laundry. Formal or conversational prayer works while running on the treadmill or walking the dog. My friend Jolene long ago started the habit of praying with her kids on the drive to school, and now that her kids are in senior high and drive themselves to school, they've kept up the habit on their own. I pray when insomnia strikes, and our family says a decade of the Rosary on the way to Mass every Sunday. Prayers for safe travel and a litany of saints kick off every road trip for us.

But *don't* get overwhelmed or scrupulous and worry that you should attach something to everything. And don't fret when you forget. ("Oh, no! I just did the laundry and all I thought about was despising laundry!") Start small. Pray, hope, and don't worry, as Padre Pio said. I guarantee you the pairings and prayers will grow.

One more note on making time for prayer: a friend of mine who has four very young children told me she has "nothing to offer" in the way of prayer advice. "If desperate pleas thrown up to God all day long counted," she said, shaking her head, "then I guess I'd have something to offer."

Yeah. They count. Mothering counts. Devotion to your babies is devotion to God. Don't forget that when your life feels insane.

Keep Doing It: Accountability, Staying On Track, and Discernment

I really need to be accountable. That's why I have a spiritual director, a best friend, and a scale.

A spiritual director is someone who will help you grow in the spiritual life through discussion and accountability. This is often a priest, but not necessarily. Generally, you meet once a month for an hour. If your director is a priest, you may or may not want him to be your confessor as well.

So how do you get a director? I asked a priest whom I considered seriously holy if he had time to be my director. He said yes. Sometimes it's that easy, but often it's not. And it doesn't always remain easy. My own relationship is complicated by the fact that my director now lives in another town. You can ask for recommendations at your parish, at the diocesan office, and at local religious communities. It takes time to discover who and what you're comfortable with, and don't feel bad if you start something that doesn't work out. You're supposed to be growing, right? If you're not, move on. Directors get that.

What if you can't find a spiritual director? I have good friends I call my *other* spiritual directors, people who know me intimately and aren't afraid to tell me when I'm doing something stupid. If you don't have that, start exploring. Is there a group in your parish of like-minded women? A mothers' group, a young adult group, something for singles, divorced or widowed? Deep friendships don't happen overnight, but finding women of similar circumstance is a great starting point. It takes just one or two friends with whom you feel an affinity. Ask if they'd like to start small. Get together for coffee, conversation, a Rosary, or whatever you're comfortable with. Give it time to grow.

Be open to flux and changing needs. For a while, I ran a moms' group at my house. In that season of life when my children were young and my brain cells needed companionship, it was a perfect outlet. But kids grow and circumstances change; I eventually eased out of the group. Be willing to explore; what worked at one time may not work forever.

A genuine spiritual friendship is a treasure; don't ever discount its value. Find healthy ways to make time for your own spiritual growth through a director, a friend, or both.

Discernment: Am I Really Making Progress? How Do I Know?

Sometimes, I'm tooling along, pretending I'm Superwoman, when I unexpectedly screech to a halt. I look around and realize I'm alone. I'm dry. I'm not really praying. I'm distant from God. When did *that* happen?

Whenever it does, my spiritual director encourages me to ask myself a simple question: "What am I doing differently?" In other words, what was I doing when I felt closer to God? What has changed? My answers vary:

- I haven't picked up a Bible in weeks.

- I stopped praying the (Breviary/Rosary/Chaplet).

- I keep watching HGTV, and I can't stop thinking about doing a room for less than $2,000.

It always comes back to the same thing: my focus, or lack of it, on my prayer life. God is faithful. Me? Not so much. If I'm not communicating with God, how can I be close to him? How can I trust someone to whom I never talk?

❀

Sometimes, I'm tooling along, pretending I'm Superwoman, when I look around and realize I'm alone. I'm dry. I'm not really praying. I'm distant from God. When did *that* happen?

❀

Should It Stay or Should It Go?

Once I've answered, "What's different?" I can form a plan of attack. I may need to reclaim a practice or jettison something.

When I was an atheist, I scoffed at nutty Christians who thought they could decipher God's will for their lives. I likened "getting an answer to prayer" to "I was beamed up to the mother ship for a quick probe before they returned me to the crop circle." Now I consider answers to prayer to be, well, answers. They're not always definitive, but they usually give me a little nudge or a bit of peace where there was anxiety. They offer me one well-lighted step forward on a path that is still inky dark up ahead.

In his book *Retreat with the Lord*, Fr. John Hardon offers simple steps for discernment based on the spiritual exercises of St. Ignatius of Loyola. St. Ignatius offered a concise discernment guide on relationships, activities, and situations, which all fall into one of these categories:

♦ Things and people God wants us to enjoy

♦ Things and people God wants us to endure (or suffer)

♦ Things and people God wants us to remove (because they lead us to sin)

♦ Things and people God wants us to sacrifice (willingly give up an objective good)

This guide isn't the certitude I pine for, but bullet points are always good, right? Usually, after prayer, reflection, and — ouch — surrender, I can see the category into which a situation falls. Not always, but sometimes. And certainly more often than I would if I weren't attempting to discern at all. This process has helped me numerous times to know whether to say yes or no to something.

"Purity of Heart Is to Will One Thing"

That quote is from Danish philosopher Soren Kierkegaard, and it's also the title of one of his books. I've posted the quote on a wall in my house because it reminds me to check in: "Am I willing the one thing today? Or are my priorities out of whack?"

Remember the movie *Moonstruck*? Olympia Dukakis is married, but on her own for the evening, having dinner alone at a restaurant. She invites John Mahoney to join her at her table when his date walks out on him. He's charmed and suggests that their brief, flirtatious dinner advance to something more. He walks her home, and when she tells him he can't come in, he thinks he knows the reason. "Because someone's home?" he asks. Her answer surprises him. "You can't come in because I know who I am."

Though my life has been full of about-faces, since my conversion I can say one thing with confidence: I know who I am. Life is still messy, but I get that the goal in life is to will one thing: loving Jesus Christ. I do that not by striving to be Superwoman, but by striving to be the Catholic woman he is calling me to be through my vocation as wife, mother, and writer.

My One Thing keeps me anchored. There will be crosses, disease, heartache, loss, loneliness, disability, dysfunction, depression, stress, and pressure. There will be doubt — though it's good to remember that doubt might be nothing more than hunger, a bad day, sleep deprivation, boredom, allergy season, or indigestion. But my One Thing — Christ — will accompany me wherever I go. And beneath the worldly turmoil, he will feed me with the soul-calming peace that comes with knowing who I am.

Who am I?

I am one of the many faces of the new rebellion, which is so perfectly summed up in the words of St. Gianna Molla: "Be living witnesses of the greatness and beauty of Christianity."

One Thing. Hang on to that, and you can take on the world.

QUESTIONS FOR REFLECTION

1. Do you pray on the run and seldom make time for formal prayer? Or, do you pray formally (Holy Mass, Rosary, other traditional prayers) but rarely feel intimate and spontaneous with God? Identify three things you can do or schedule in the coming week or month to help tip the scales toward more balance in your prayer life.

2. Think about a time when you were very close to the Lord and all felt right with the world. What was happening in your life at that time? What is different now?

3. Who is your favorite saint or most admired spiritual hero? Read and learn as much as you can about that person; choose one thing from his or her life to emulate. Find some quotes by or about your hero and post them someplace convenient (home, car, office, computer) so that you will be reminded of your hero's virtues on a daily basis.

4. Edith Stein said that we "must go to the world in order to carry the divine life into it." When you are in the world, how are you carrying the divine life? When you're "in the world" are you "of it"? How can you best balance inner devotion and deep faith with constant worldly interaction?

5. Using Fr. Hardon's discernment questions (see Page 52), take stock of the activities and people in your life. Is everything in order? What should stay? What should go?

6. *What is your "one thing"? Is your life ordered around the one thing that is most important to you? Identify key areas that feel unbalanced or cause you to feel you are shortchanging your one thing. How would you answer the question, "Who are you?"*

Karen Edmisten, a convert from atheism, is the author of *The Rosary: Keeping Company with Jesus and Mary*, *Through the Year With Mary: 365 Reflections*, and *After Miscarriage*. A popular blogger, Karen is also a regular guest on Relevant Radio. Find her online at www.karenedmisten.com.

CHAPTER 4

Sex, Passion, and Purity

Elizabeth Duffy

My husband and I are in our mid-to-late thirties. We're practicing Catholics who don't use birth control. We've had five kids, two miscarriages, eleven years of peaceable marriage, and lots of fun in the bedroom. To our happy surprise, the sex only gets better as the years go by, which makes you wonder, because it wasn't too terrible to begin with.

There have been a few bumps in the road along the way.

I used to think that marriage took care of all the issues surrounding sex. No more temptation, no more questions about how far is too far, no more guilt about impure relationships, no more lonely nights. Sex problems solved. I didn't realize that getting married is just the beginning. We still had a lot to learn about how to live out our sexual relationship in the light of God's blessing.

Dating, Dignity, and Christ

Before marriage, however, there were all those years of dating when questions regarding sex were on my mind, as they are for so many women. Very few young women, Catholic or otherwise, make it through adolescence in the twenty-first century without at least one episode we wish never happened. Maybe it was only a kiss, maybe masturbation, maybe we had sex with a high school boyfriend, or several boyfriends.

When one bad relationship follows another, as it did for me, it can seem that virtuous men are a made-up ideal existing only in books, monasteries, or marriages, always just out of reach. Dabbling in sin, however, only illuminates how degrading the world's ways can be, piling jadedness and disappointment on top of self-loathing when we give ourselves to anything less than the deepest longing of our heart, life lived in union with God.

Once I developed a relationship with Christ, I was amazed by the inherent dignity and worth I found in his true love. Christ listens to our arguments, but doesn't fight back. He doesn't lie, pressure, or humiliate us. Having a relationship with him doesn't require any compromise with virtue. If there is a way to live chastely as a single woman — and there is — it's through him.

And yet, I still struggled with chastity. I knew sex before marriage was wrong, but I didn't know what was considered appropriate physical contact. Many of us grew up thinking that anything goes, as long as you don't have sex. But if anything goes, sex often follows. "How far is too far?"

I never wanted to feel God's absence in my life again, so I knew I needed strong boundaries. Here are some tips that helped me set limits and might help others negotiating the dating scene:

- ◆ Chastity is a lifestyle, not a decision made in the heat of the moment. Replace negative influences on chastity with relationships, situations, and environments that support the decision for Christ.

- ◆ As the *Catechism of the Catholic Church* says: "Chastity includes an *apprenticeship in self-mastery* which is a training in human freedom. The alternative is clear: either man governs his passions and finds peace, or he lets himself be dominated by them and becomes unhappy" (2339).

- ◆ Alcohol rarely has a positive effect on budding relationships. It doesn't make sense to hang out in bars looking for guys if we want to date someone with shared Christian values.

- ◆ Developing relationships with strong Christian women holds us accountable. It also helps us connect with a wider social circle that includes Christian men.

- ◆ Submitting to parent-approved behaviors doesn't threaten our independence. It supports freedom from sin.

- ◆ Prayer and frequent reception of the sacraments — especially the Eucharist and reconciliation — always help, even when we feel nothing.

In past dating relationships, I relied on my own strength to reason my way through trials rather than drawing strength from God. Then I felt deflated when my own strength wasn't enough. I thought there was an on/off switch by which God loved me one day and hated me the next. Committing a serious sin cut me off; going to confession flipped the switch back on. Without a *relationship* with God, we are graceless creatures attempting to live by arbitrary standards. Such extremism can only leave us exhausted and discouraged.

Engagement: Building Companionship

My husband was the black sheep of his family — the only one of four brothers who didn't spend time in a Catholic seminary. But he knew the faith, and together we decided we would do things differently than we had in the past.

We met for Mass after work. In the evenings, if the smooching got too hot and heavy, we'd stop to say the Rosary. Anything beyond kissing was a danger zone for us. We put a strategic plan in place to help us avoid sex before our wedding. Both of us had a gut feeling that God had chosen us, one for the other, and we wanted to honor his plan by staying faithful to his teaching.

Dating chastely, we were free to be at ease, to play, to be companions rather than lovers. We went for walks, made dinners, and hung out with our families. Our engagement was one of the happiest years of my life, and with the help of the sacraments our wedding night was the first time we were together.

But the fight for chastity was not complete. As the *Catechism* says: "Self-mastery is a *long and exacting work*. One can never consider it acquired once and for all. It presupposes renewed effort at all stages of life" (2342). It's been many years and numerous trips to the confessional since then. Marriage is not a free pass against mortal sin; sexuality is always in need of a Redeemer. We all fail in loving generously, in abstaining prudently, in respecting one another appropriately.

As my children begin their own apprenticeship in self-mastery, I often tell them that we don't dodge guilt or shame by redefining sin or redirecting blame. We overcome shame only through the goodness, mercy, and forgiveness of God. Jesus tells us to "Go and learn what this means, 'I desire mercy, and not sacrifice.' For I came not to call the righteous, but sinners" (Mt 9:13, RSV).

It is less important that we perform perfectly in our sexual apprenticeship than that we remain beggars before our God who saves. Again and again, we beg God for guidance, for strength, for prudence, for charity. We beg him to make us holy, and we persevere when we make mistakes.

Establishing Sexual Trust

Engaging in a sexual relationship in the context of the sacrament of marriage illuminated the damaging effects of sex outside of marriage. I hung my life on my husband's fidelity, but I knew he would go to work and see prettier, more outgoing women than I. In the past, an ex-boyfriend blindsided me by living a double life, and I was petrified it could happen again. Demon memories from past relationships had begun to rear their heads.

Before marriage, I knew my sins hurt my own soul, but I didn't realize they could hurt my spouse, the women my old boyfriends ultimately married, their children, and my children. This is my primary argument to the unmarried woman struggling with chastity: Sin has social consequences that reverberate throughout families, cultures, and generations. God forgives sin, but its effects live on, either through jealousy of a spouse's former flames, or through unwanted memories of our own.

Nevertheless, we can't allow the past to undo a marriage. There's no overnight cure for problems years in the making, but there are ways to lessen the effects of the past on our marriage:

◆ Realize that fear of this nature is usually from the devil. Fear of being hurt, left behind, unloved, lied to, abandoned — it often comes from the devil who loves to destroy good marriages. Reject fear.

◆ Put trust in the divine mercy of Jesus. No sin outweighs God's mercy. If you have been to confession and repented of sin, God has given you a clean slate. Ask also for freedom from jealousy or negative memories.

◆ Trust in God's plan for your life. We can't preempt infidelity or accidents by living our lives always waiting for the other shoe to drop. But we can drive our husbands crazy with lack of trust and suspicion. If one loses a spouse to infidelity or death, God will provide the grace to carry on.

◆ Pray for people who have hurt you. It's tempting to indulge in anger toward people from our past who contributed to a loss of innocence, or to feel pleasure in the thought that they might be suffering. To become free of the past, we have to build Christ's kingdom of love and mercy, rather than heaping hurtful thoughts onto sinful actions that took place long ago. Whenever a troubling memory arises regarding an ex, say a quick prayer for the guy involved, his spouse, and their children. Praying for our husbands' exes, too, can be a liberating experience.

Natural Family Planning

My husband and I never quibbled with the Church's teaching on birth control, but we achieved pregnancy on our honeymoon, and again and again, nearly every time conception was possible. I was afraid I might be pregnant for the rest of my life. I knew babies were a blessing and part of God's plan for marriage, but I needed some breathing room.

Before marriage, I thought that sex was a right for married people, an all-you-can-eat sex buffet. My husband and I gorged at that buffet for the first two years of marriage, and then we felt sick. I resented him because sex didn't have the same risks for him. Pregnancy made sex painful sometimes and decreased my drive, so I often put him in the position of begging for sex that I made clear I was in no mood to enjoy. ("Mind if I read a book while you do that?") We had figured out how to procreate, but the sexual pleasure was often one-sided, and it was hardly uniting.

I had the four-hundred page handbook on natural family planning, but I was thoroughly confused by all the signs and symbols, and with two very young kids I could never get my temperature taken before I did anything else in the morning. Plus, mucus is gross. I wanted to stay as far away from mucus as I could and still figure out what was going on. It's not possible.

In order to be comfortable having intimacy with my husband, we needed to master natural family planning, so we signed up for a class. Learning NFP was definitely a blessing for our marriage. It took a bit of practice and counseling from our NFP coaches to find the best method for us, but the benefits were many.

For a Catholic, sexuality is a constant reckoning of bodily realities to spiritual ones. Christ became man in the Incarnation, fully human, fully divine. I've always wondered why people say the Catholic Church makes people feel shameful about their bodies. Natural family planning puts a woman on very intimate terms with her anatomy and helps to prepare her for the often intimate care she will provide for her babies and other family members in need of help with hygiene.

After I had given birth a couple times, certain signposts of fertility become both easier to reach and to read. Sensitivity to these signs deepens one's understanding of the cyclical renewal of the body and can draw the practitioner of NFP into a heightened awareness of the similar themes of sloughing and renewal, fasting and feasting, echoed in the Church calendar. One thing that becomes clear when a couple learns NFP is that sex itself is a gift. Just as fasting from food helps to illuminate attachments in our life that have displaced God, times of fasting from sex can bring to light weaknesses that a couple needs to address, like finding nonsexual means of communication and expressing affection. By abstaining for a couple of weeks out of the cycle, sex becomes something that we *get* to do rather than something we *have* to do.

Finally, NFP brings husbands into a verbal dialogue about sex, rather than allowing them to just use sex itself to communicate. They can recognize natural fluctuations in their wives' libido because of ovulation and take heart that their apparent disinterest in sex at times is hormonal rather than a personal rejection. Many husbands also note that being apart helps them better appreciate times of togetherness.

Rediscovering Love

When things are dull in the bedroom, some might be tempted to turn to worldly sources that promise good sex. These include not only sexy movies and pornographic websites (into which faithful Catholics dare not go), but also the supposedly less harmful outlets such as women's magazines that provide explicit tips for how to please your man, or yourself, often in ways that don't jive with biblical principles. Lingerie stores promise good sex with the purchase of a sixty-dollar bra. Novelty stores sell board games that encourage sexual bartering. Sex is always for sale.

And yet the most satisfying sex occurs when couples are best friends — and friendship is something you cannot buy. My husband and I have always positioned our bed under a window, and one summer night the bats were out, flying very close to our screen. We both jumped up on our knees to look out the window. It felt like we were two children, suspended for a moment by our mutual fascination in something other than ourselves — matrimonial innocence, like two lovers before the fall. It was just a little taste of the sweetness that ensues when we quit treating each other like a trick pony: *I'm here. Talk to me. Other couples talk. Why don't we?* If we can look outward together, we are bound and united by our mutual experiences and labors. Maybe we don't need to talk so much.

I don't want to be his sex kitten any more than he wants to be my Fabio. And I don't want my husband remade into the fantastic image I've created of The Perfect Catholic Man. I fell in love with *him*, his personality, his sense of humor, his quirks, his strengths. It helps to concentrate on the reasons you love your husband rather than the reasons he gets on your nerves, because in addition to good sex, you want a good *relationship*.

A good relationship, however, doesn't mean you are co-dependent clones of one another. Before marriage, my husband and I were separate people with separate identities and interests. I enjoyed being with him, treasured his opinions, and shared my own thoughts with charity rather than with shredding derision about the ways he was failing to serve me.

Marriage makes us one and unites us in this vocation of raising a family together, but maintaining interests and friendships that we cherished before marriage removes some of the pressure to be everything for the other. It also provides enough variation in time spent apart that we have things to discuss when we spend time together. It goes without saying, however, that we want to be chosen over our husband's other activities and hobbies, and our husbands want to be chosen over ours, and so we have to guard against making idols of those things. In the hierarchy of values, Christ comes first, then our marriage and kids. Our work, friendships, and hobbies follow. It's easy to lose perspective and give that which is easiest and most enjoyable too high a place on the scale of values.

The Pleasure Principle

After conducting an informal survey of a group of Catholic women, I've concluded that many of us downplay the importance of our own pleasure in the married relationship. It's easy to do. At the end of a day spent meeting the needs of our children or the demands of our jobs, our husbands can seem like one more person who wants something from us. We may feel tempted to fake climax, or to give up and get it over with.

But we are not running a sex charity here.

In the First Letter to the Corinthians we read: "Do not refuse one another except perhaps by agreement for a season, that you may devote yourselves to prayer; but then come together again, lest Satan tempt you through lack of self-control" (1 Cor 7:5, RSV). When a couple abstains periodically for NFP or after having baby, many wives rightly challenge themselves to respond to every overture their husband makes when they're not abstaining. But the passage above says "do not refuse *one another*," which means that he also must be responsive to his wife's needs.

We need our spouse's support financially and emotionally. We need his protection for ourselves and for our children. We need relaxation and companionship. But we also need to foster a sex life that is mutually self-giving and mutually enjoyable, or we may be overwhelmed by negative feelings toward our husbands and sex. Satan not only tempts people to stray from their marriages, but also to hate the acts that can help bring couples together.

Though there are times in life for the occasional "quickie," giving up on finding pleasure in sex is not an option. In his book *Love and Responsibility*, Pope John Paul II warns against creating a marital culture that consents to the use of persons. Repeatedly omitting our own pleasure in sex is a tacit consent to being used, even if we have generous intent.

A woman finds it very difficult to forgive a man if she derives no satisfaction from intercourse. It becomes difficult to endure this, and as the years go her resentment may grow out of all proportion to the cause. This may lead to the collapse of the marriage.[6]

A satisfying sex life increases the bond we feel with our husband, a bond that is necessary for the marriage to thrive, because in Christian marriage sex is more than just the exchange of bodily fluids. It's a renewal of our marriage vows. Not every sexual encounter will be a spiritually profound experience, but our hearts should be in the act as much as our bodies.

While some couples may have difficulty reaching a simultaneous climax, the burden is on the husband to ensure his wife's climax. We should not feel selfish for seeking this pleasure or making a commitment with our husbands to work on what makes us tick.

❦❦

We are adept at anticipating impending crosses. It's the resurrection we're so bad at predicting — the blessing of relationships with Christ, with our spouse, with a yet unknown child, the blessing of a peaceful interior relationship with ourselves.

❦❦

Sexual Preparation

We have to prepare not only to give ourselves to our husbands, but also to receive them. Silence negative thinking. Reflect on his best attributes. Ask God for the grace of holy desire, for the gift of pleasure and relaxation. Thank him for the gift of your husband and your marriage.

Address housekeeping and hygiene issues in advance of potential intimacy. We may be able to tune out a messy house, but the bedroom isn't negotiable. It's our sanctuary in more than just a decorate-in-soothing-colors way. Even if we can't get the clean clothes put away, it helps to make the bed every day, pick up the dirty laundry, and change the sheets when necessary.

It sounds pitiful that hygiene is one of the most difficult issues for me to address as a wife and mother. If I don't have plans that take me out of the house, showering and tooth-brushing often occur later, if ever. I don't like the idea of being Betty Homemaker, always in a skirt with a bow in her hair, ready to go when her husband wants to take her to bed. I am not that passive woman. But I don't have to be stubborn about it, either.

Think of hygiene as an act of seduction rather than an act of submission. *Smell me, I'm minty! Kiss me and you won't be sorry. I'm getting in the shower — wanna come too?* Not to mention, it just feels better to take care of ourselves.

After all the practical stuff — housekeeping, hygiene, positive thinking — it doesn't hurt to go the extra mile: flirt with the man.

One night I brought the book *His Needs, Her Needs* into bed. "Why don't we read this book?" I said to my husband. "It comes highly recommended by many of my relatives."

"Like who?" he asked.

"Like my mom. And also by many psychotherapists. See, they say on the back it will make your marriage sizzle. We could read a chapter a night."

"I know how to make our marriage sizzle," he said. "Why don't you read a chapter out loud to me right now — naked?"

Naked reading wasn't exactly what I had in mind. But it raised a good point: if you want to improve your sex life, good intentions are not enough. You have to be willing to be vulnerable, open, and adaptable. Willing to face any darkness under the surface of your marriage, and also willing to laugh.

We are body and soul, and as such equally concerned with the humanity of our sex lives as we are with the spiritual side of things. In many Catholic books that discuss sex, you'll find words like "connubial embrace" and "marital act" — words that elevate sex to heavenly heights no mortal can breach. While sex is no joke, let's also not take it too seriously. Any time two adults proceed in a game of Twister, they'll need a sense of humor.

Here are some ideas to put the fun back in funny business:

◆ If you have a lot of very young kids to put to bed, or any toddlers who won't stay in bed, waiting until after hours for sex will ensure that both of you are too tired and frustrated to do anything. Try having a family nap time when your husband gets home from work, or put a movie on the TV for the kids, lock the doors, and do it while you still have some energy.

◆ When your husband says he's going to go sleep in the hammock or in the tent (insert annoying-place-to-sleep of choice), and would you like to join him, the answer is *yes*. At least for a little while. Even if you only lie there and experience the novelty with him for a few minutes and then go back inside to your comfy bed, give it a whirl and see what happens.

◆ On greenlight nights, sleep naked. You don't have to do anything but feel each other's skin. Sometimes saying that you're not going to have sex is an enticement to actually having it. It increases sexual tension, which can be a turn-on.

◆ Conversely, if you know sex is on the menu, make your husband work a little harder to get your clothes off. Kiss and kiss some more before he gets to take off your underthings.

◆ If you're unevenly yoked temperaturewise, be partially dressed. Sometimes it's appealing to leave things to the imagination.

In spite of all these preparations, there will still be times when sex is distracted and disappointing. No matter what anyone else says about all the great sex they're having, sometimes great sex eludes us. There's no need to dwell on it or assign blame, but if there's an ongoing problem, address it.

———————◆◆◆◆◆———————

Finding sexual balance is really a search for peace — peace that comes from maintaining friendship with Christ, peace when body and soul are united, and peace with the world around us when we can turn an open and loving face to the people in our lives.

We are adept at anticipating impending crosses. It's the resurrection we're so bad at predicting — the blessing of relationships with Christ, with our spouse, with a yet unknown child, the blessing of a peaceful interior relationship with ourselves, a life that is overflowing with so many opportunities to love and be loved. A life filled with the gifts of doing God's will.

QUESTIONS FOR REFLECTION

1. At what stage am I in my sexual apprenticeship? Am I still struggling with chastity? Are there aspects of the Church's teaching that are difficult for me to accept? And if so, do I seek Jesus in the sacraments as a source of peace and strength, or do I prefer argument?

2. Do I entertain fears about sex, sin, the past, or my husband's fidelity that inhibit my being intimate with him? Do I believe that Jesus forgives my sins, heals my spirit, and eliminates fear from my life? Are there any unresolved sexual issues in my life that might need the support of a spiritual director, confessor, or medical professional?

3. What misconceptions have I entertained about how a married sex life should look? Do I compare my sex life with those of my friends or with examples I see in movies and magazines?

4. Am I doing my part to foster an intimate relationship with my husband, or do I expect him to make everything work out for us?

a. Throughout the day, am I addressing basic housekeeping and hygiene issues that might be an obstacle to sex?

b. On good days for intimacy, do I go the extra mile to put myself in the mood for sex? Examples: kissing my husband, thinking positively about our relationship, relishing the good he does for our family, feeling grateful for God's gifts? Often the biggest enemy to a good sex life is resentment and ingratitude. Am I nurturing those negative attitudes?

5. *Do I ever create negative scenarios in order to avoid having sex? These include picking fights on days I know my husband might be interested or bringing up difficult discussion topics right before bed. How can I make sure my husband and I discuss important issues without dumping on him at bedtime? At bedtime, do I habitually put "things" before my relationship with my husband: last-minute chores, reading, scanning the Internet, or watching other media?*

6. *If I have difficulty enjoying sex, am I able to verbalize why? Am I comfortable communicating the problem to myself? My husband? Is there a female friend or relative in my life to whom I can turn for trustworthy council about making sex more enjoyable?*

Elizabeth (Betty) Duffy is a freelance writer and author of a faith, family, and culture column for *Patheos*. Her writing has appeared online at *Faith & Family Magazine*, the *Korrektiv Press* blog, and numerous other venues. She also authors the personal blog "Betty Duffy" at http://bettyduffy.blogspot.com. She and her husband live in rural Indiana with their five children.

CHAPTER 5

Single and Seeking God's Plan

Anna Mitchell

I'm in my late twenties now. I've been a bridesmaid eight times and watched many more friends than that head to the altar. Several of my friends have discerned a vocation to the religious life, and I've even dealt with some crushes choosing to go to seminary. I'm also feeling a bit singled out in writing this: every other woman contributing to this book is married.

Am I jealous? Absolutely. I won't sugarcoat the frustration that comes from waiting for a vocation to be realized. I am at least consoled in knowing that my ideas for the ideal life are not as good as God's. There are some major challenges — and some major blessings, too — for those of us wanting to live our lives for God while our vocation unfolds.

Our Vocation to Love

For most single people, this state in life is temporary. But even if it's not, our job right now and always is to live out the universal vocation to love. Everyone is created by Love for love, and we never lose that first calling.

Pope John Paul II wrote a lot about our call to love, and much of his writing on the human person is inspired by a passage in the Second Vatican Council's *Gaudium et Spes*: "man ... cannot truly find himself except through a sincere gift of himself."[7] We should always be working toward that goal, and we had better live our universal vocation in a way that can get us to heaven. Blessed Chiara Luce Badano, who died young (and, incidentally, unmarried), once said, "I have nothing left, but I still have my heart, and with that I can always love."[8] This should be our attitude, as well, even if we feel dismayed about our current state in life.

It is easy to fall into the temptation to live merely for ourselves, but we need to be careful to resist it and to do our best to live selflessly. And this can come about when we are committed to the pursuit of personal holiness. As one priest put it to me: If we are working on our universal call to holiness, we will be better prepared to say "yes" when God does reveal his plans for us. Why should we ask for our specific vocation if we are not willing to pursue the general vocation to holiness and prayer?

Discernment

As I write this, I have no idea whether God is calling me to marriage or to religious life. At this point I'm of the attitude that I will not rule out the convent until I'm married, but I've always leaned toward being a wife and mother. This inclination became stronger when a trusted friend who is a priest told me that it's a good assumption that I'm called to be married because God is already using me in a unique way through my career in Catholic media — which probably means that he has me where he wants me and doesn't want me to leave for a convent.

I said as much to a new priest at my parish who was rather inquisitive about my self-evaluation, and several weeks later he asked to meet with me. The meeting started off as a discussion about our young adult group, but when we exhausted that topic, he paused and said, "Now I want to talk about your vocation." Guerilla tactics. So we launched into a conversation about the religious life.

Father brought up my long-standing belief that I'm called to marriage: Even though he's a fan of St. Josemaria Escriva (the founder of Opus Dei) and subscribes to the serve-God-in-whatever-you-do mentality, he told me that this does not necessarily mean that God isn't calling me to something greater than my present course.

"So," he said, "what do you think?"

I had to admit to him that I had never *actively* discerned this option, and that it had never seemed like a real possibility in my life until I read the *Theology of the Body*, Pope John Paul II's lectures on the bodily and spiritual nature of the human person. The idea of religious life being eschatological — that is, vowed to God on earth as we will be in heaven — was appealing to me. However, I learned about it at an inopportune time, when I was dealing with quite a bit of hardship. I told him that it would be difficult to determine whether the religious way of life was attractive to me for what it was, or because I just wanted to escape to a convent.

After listening for a while, Father agreed that I didn't quite have all my ducks in a row to discern a call to religious life. He went on to explain that according to St. Alphonsus Liguori, there are five indications that God could be calling a person to don a habit. Let's go through what he told me:

♦ **Knowledge.** Father brought up the example of a friend who had decided that he wanted to be a monk. When asked what a monk does, he replied that he didn't know, but was looking forward to not having to work. This friend probably wasn't called to be a monk, because he didn't have enough knowledge of the vocation to make that judgment.

♦ **Desire.** Once you know about the religious way of life, you must *want* it. Actually, Father explained, it's not merely a wish — but something closer to intention. You have to see it as a good, and specifically as a good for *you*.

♦ **Right circumstances.** You must be able to go freely and completely. If you are bound by something, whether it be debt (a big issue for many who desire religious life), family circumstances, health, and so forth, then the timing isn't ideal. This doesn't mean that you aren't ultimately called to religious life — only that you are not ready *yet*.

♦ **Spiritual direction.** This is essential: You must have the advice of a priest or spiritual director *who knows you* and knows your circumstances. It is almost impossible to step back and be objective about your own life as you determine whether this is the right choice to make. A trusted spiritual adviser can help you sort through and under-stand everything.

- ◆ **Acceptance into an order.** We often overlook the fact that religious life is a two-way street, and the orders must also discern that you are a good fit with them. If you apply to the Dominican Sisters but have no desire to teach, for example, or if you apply to a cloister but want to work with the poor, you will probably be encouraged to apply to another order with a charism that better matches your talents and aspirations.

Once Father laid this out, it was clear that I did not meet the third requirement, and that he did not meet the fourth, at least not yet. He told me that he was glad to know all this and that now he would pray for me. He encouraged me to continue praying, too, and (only half tongue-in-cheek) to say, "God, I will continue to carry my cross; I look forward to seeing where you will have me crucified."

Dating

There seem to be two camps in the world of Catholic dat-ing advice. Let's call them the courtship camp and the take-matters-into-your-own-hands camp (TMIYOH camp, for short). Some people are fully entrenched in one or the other of these two sides; and then there are the rest of us who end up somewhere in the middle.

The courtship camp members are committed to the idea that the man should lead. They take seriously the mandate in the fifth chapter of Ephesians regarding the mutual submis-sion between spouses (wives submit to their husbands while husbands lay down their lives for their wives), and they extend this idea into the world of courtship. I say courtship because many don't like to use the word *dating*. The courtship camp says that because the man should naturally be in the lead, he should be the one to initiate a relationship. For some, there is little-to-no physical affection, both to avoid temptation and to save all for your spouse alone. I have to say, though I don't subscribe to everything they promote, those whom I know in this camp seem to end up in very holy marriages.

The TMIYOH camp members take a more aggressive approach to dating — and they *do* call it dating. The main idea behind their philosophy is that times have changed, women are more independent, men have become less confident, and so it's not wrong for women to take the initiative. It is perfectly acceptable to openly flirt with a guy you want to get to know and, if necessary, to invite him on some innocuous date to try to spark interest and encourage him. The TMIYOH campers also highly encourage young women to be active in the online dating scene, because it is the easiest way to expand the pool of potential mates.

Those like me who are not of either persuasion put together a strategy borrowing ideas from both. What follows is my hodgepodge philosophy of dating. But take it for what it's worth. I'm mindful of a scene in the *Music Man* when Marian's mom, singing to the tune of the piano-lesson scales, wonders why a married woman would ever take advice from a single woman no matter how smart and able to quote Balzac and Shakespeare the single woman might be. The same point applies here: Because I don't have a husband, why listen to me? So I've asked some trusted advisers (who will remain anonymous) to give me advice. You'll find, below, some of what I liked from them, as well as some original thoughts based on my own misadventures in dating.

To begin, I much prefer for a guy to ask me out. I do believe there is a place for traditional dating values in this modern world, and I don't like the idea of initiating a relationship, no matter how casual. That being said, I think it's important to make sure a guy knows that you're interested. I particularly regret, for example, not taking advantage of a small advance from a very nice, handsome, and faithful young man who gave me his phone number in an e-mail after I met him. I, being ultra-traditionalist at the time, wanted him to explicitly ask for my phone number before I'd give it to him. I never offered it in subsequent email exchanges, nor did I call him. The result: Emails became scarce, and I started worrying that we'd lose contact altogether. I finally called him, and he did call me back, but by then we were friends and nothing more.

If you are in a relationship, affection is necessary. Otherwise, how is a guy to know that you think of him as anything more than a friend? But, of course, we need to be careful. The virtue of chastity doesn't merely involve abstaining from sex before marriage — it's the refusal to objectify another person. My basic philosophy is that you need to know where to draw the morally acceptable line, and then you must not cross it. And for heaven's sake don't have sex before marriage! I hope I'm preaching to the choir in this regard because we all know it's wrong. One friend said to keep in mind that "chastity is much harder to keep when you're dating someone who's not of the same faith, or at least of the same mind about sex."

High expectations are always dangerous, and it's wrong to judge men based on "marriageability." Dating shouldn't be frivolous; it should always be directed toward marriage, but don't reject an upstanding guy outright just because you can't immediately imagine him in a tux standing next to you in a white dress. Two friends told me almost simultaneously, "Lists are stupid." One mentioned she might have never considered her husband if she had made a list when she was younger. She said, "If you must have a list, I think that the most important attributes for a spouse to have are (in this order) that they be: 1. humble; 2. reasonable; and 3. Catholic." (A bonus tip from her, because there's nowhere else to put it: "If you get drunk all the time, this will lead to problems in your dating life." Duly noted).

There may be a lot that you don't know about a person, no matter how much you think you have him pegged. Further, much refining can happen for *both* of you before either of you is ready to marry. Think of Elizabeth Bennet in *Pride and Prejudice*. At one point in the story she tells Mr. Darcy, "And I had not known you a month before I felt that you were the last man in the world whom I could ever be prevailed upon to marry." How'd that work out for her? One friend had a similar real-life experience: "I thought he was dull — I wanted someone more outgoing, more artsy, more romantic. Of course, all the dudes I picked out were idiots. When I finally got around to dating my husband— and really got to know him (it took way more than one date, more like five or six to know him) — I couldn't believe how wrong I'd been."

Speaking of expectations, don't start to plan your wedding the minute you find the man of your dreams — especially if he hasn't asked you out yet. Whenever I find myself fantasizing about the future, I remind myself of the section in C.S. Lewis's *The Screwtape Letters* that says the present is the time that touches eternity, so if you want to pull someone away from eternity, get them to think only about the future. I have fallen prey to this more times than I'd like to admit. We women are so easily drawn into girlish romantic fantasies. It's not fair to the men who are expected to deliver these unrealistic expectations, nor is it fair to us. Protect your heart!

꿰

Dating shouldn't be frivolous; it should always be directed toward marriage, but don't reject an upstanding guy outright just because you can't immediately imagine him in a tux standing next to you in a white dress.

꿰

Dealing with Loneliness

Perhaps the hardest thing about being single is dealing with loneliness. I grew up privileged to know two great-aunts who were wonderful, faith-filled women who never married and lived together until they died. Though they led exemplary lives, I imagine that they sometimes dealt with loneliness and probably some occasional regret for never marrying.

I'm still young, but I have struggled with loneliness. My heart goes out to all the God-fearing men and women who have waited longer than I, or who have felt the call to marriage but have never realized their vocation. There's no real explanation for why, and it just doesn't seem fair.

No one likes to be lonely, but we shouldn't ignore the feeling. We can use it for good. Our suffering can mean something, and it can be used for a spiritual purpose. Give your loneliness to God. Offer it up for the salvation of souls in Purgatory, or for the conversion of someone you know, or in reparation for your own sins. I like the idea of offering it to God for the holiness of your future husband.

Rely on your friends, but not too much. Don't fill up your life with friend-time — and I know this from experience — because you'll start depending on them more than you depend on God, and you will also run the risk of coming off as someone more interested in your friends than in a boyfriend. That being said, friends are indispensible in keeping you from becoming an island.

Pursue your career, but don't become a workaholic. It's the same idea as with friendship: You need to keep busy, and you need to support yourself. (You also need to use the gifts God gave you to bring his life into the workplace.) But keep it in perspective. If you're working all the time, you'll never meet anyone but co-workers.

Don't wear loneliness on your sleeve. There's a reason that "comforting the afflicted" is a spiritual work of mercy: it's painful and tiresome to be with them! Beyond that, Jesus instructs us to anoint our heads and wash our faces when we fast, and I think the same principle holds true when dealing with loneliness. God knows your suffering, and your Father who sees this in secret will reward you. If you look for sympathy elsewhere, you have already been repaid.

Remember: "For I know well the plans I have in mind for you…plans for your welfare and not for woe, so as to give you a future of hope" (Jer 29:11, NABRE). I couldn't tell you why I am single right now, but I know God has a plan. There are so many times I've questioned why things were happening the way they were, and then later I would look back and see how God's hand was working. I often have to remind myself to trust God. His plans are always better than mine.

Keep in mind that for most of us this single state is just temporary. There's a prayer I try to pray every day that says (among a great many other things), "I want to do what you ask of me: in the way you ask, for as long as you ask, because you ask it." If God wants me to be single for a little while longer, so be it. I need to learn to die to self, follow his will and do what I can with this current freedom to further his kingdom.

One of my favorite quotes comes from St. Thérèse of Lisieux: "I have always wanted to become a saint. Unfortunately when I have compared myself with the saints, I have always found that there is the same difference between the saints and me as there is between a mountain whose summit is lost in the clouds and a humble grain of sand trodden underfoot by passersby. Instead of being discouraged, I told myself: God would not make me wish for something impossible and so, in spite of my littleness, I can aim at being a saint."[9]

St. Thérèse was talking about the pursuit of holiness specifically, but we who are single and don't want to be single can take heart thinking about the idea that God doesn't inspire unrealistic desires. We must spend time pursuing God. We must be persistent in asking for our vocation, and — this is key — asking that he conform us to *his* will. It is only then that we will always receive what we want — his plan for our life.

We must have a selfless and persistent love for God.

That, single women, is our challenge.

QUESTIONS FOR REFLECTION

1. As a single person, what are your biggest obstacles to your pursuit of personal holiness? Have you ever let your struggles get the best of you? How and why?

2. What are some practical ways that you can overcome these obstacles? For what can you be grateful right now? How can you give of yourself as a single woman?

3. Could God be calling you to religious life? Have you ever actively discerned religious life? Where do you line up on the Alphonsus Liguori checklist?

4. What are you doing to meet people? What are your dating techniques? Do you think they are appropriate and fruitful? Where do you draw the line with a guy physically?

5. Who can you trust for good advice about dating and relationships?

6. How will you offer up loneliness, should you experience it?

Anna Mitchell is the news director at Sacred Heart Radio and anchor for the *Son Rise Morning Show* on the EWTN Global Catholic Radio Network. She is a young adult contributor for the *Integrated Catholic Life* emagazine. She graduated from Ohio University in 2006 with degrees in journalism and history. Anna lives in Cincinnati and loves reading, writing, playing guitar, and watching Cincinnati Reds baseball, Ohio State football, and *Project Runway*.

CHAPTER 6

What Works For You?

Rebecca Ryskind Teti

I love Christmas, but I hate the way Catholics have taken to talking about it.

Not the Church herself, mind you. I mean contemporary Catholic culture, as we live it. At the first whiff of Advent, Christianity's stern-eyed aunts emerge to chant their dirges: The Christmas displays are too early and secularized. Someone said, "Season's Greetings!" Fie!

They're correct in a certain respect, but it's a dubious skill to be able to distill the astonishing news that a Savior is born who will deliver us from death down to, "You're doing it wrong."

For similar reasons, I love what the Church says to us about the unique work of women, but sometimes marvel at our capacity to turn a liberating teaching into a stifling set of expectations that make all kinds of lovely Catholic women — people who love Christ and his Church and sincerely try to live as Christians in the world — perpetually anguished that they may be doing "it" wrong — "it" being womanhood and

Catholicism. Women at home worry that they aren't making enough contribution to their families and society. Women at work fear that they're neglecting their families or, if they're single, wonder whether their careers will continue to be fulfilling and what their place is within the family of the Church. What can the watching world think to see Catholic women so unsettled?

I'm delighted, therefore, to be invited to contribute a chapter about working women to this volume. As any stay-at-home mom would tell you instantly if the topic arose, all women are working women. I thereby give myself leave not to write about office life or career fulfillment per se, and certainly not to be so presumptuous as to tell anyone else what she should be doing, but to think about women's work more broadly, and how we might make peace with where Providence has placed us as individuals within the work of women today.

No One Needs a Copycat

I'm haunted by a question that French historian Régine Pernoud poses at the conclusion of *Women in the Days of the Cathedrals:*

> Copying is a good school exercise. It has never produced a masterpiece. Why do we women not invent solutions adapted to our own time, just as other women did in their time? Have we nothing original to propose to the world, for example, when we face the grave deficiencies that torment it?[10]

She was addressing the current effort to eradicate injustice toward women by having them live exactly as men.

Couldn't we ask the same question, though, of those who try to meet the challenges posed to Christians today with a return to formulas from some vaunted golden age of Christendom or some abstract ideal? Christ is eternal, and so are the truths of faith, but culture changes over time, and each generation of Christians must find a way to re-propose Christ and the Church in a way its neighbors can hear.

In our time or any time, the ordinary way a person encounters Christ is not through explicit teaching but in the goodness of some Christian who touches his heart. During a recent pilgrimage to Fátima, Pope Benedict XVI made this very point to bishops:

> The courageous and integral appeal to principles is essential and indispensable; yet simply proclaiming the message does not penetrate to the depths of people's hearts, it does not touch their freedom, it does not change their lives. What attracts is, above all, the encounter with believing persons who, through their faith, draw others to the grace of Christ by bearing witness to him.[11]

It's not the form our work takes that's decisive, in other words, but who we are while we're working. A person who knows Jesus intimately through prayer and the sacraments will have more spiritual energy, more insight into what her priorities should be, and will radiate his goodness in ways she's not even aware to the people she meets each day, be they husband, kids, neighbors, colleagues, or friends at the bar.

It Has Nothing to Do with Pink

This "radiation" of Christ into every sector of society, teaching the human person his innate worth and dignity in God's eyes, is the work of the Church as a whole and all Christians, men and women alike. It's particularly entrusted to women, however, because God has written into their being the "feminine genius" and a universal call to motherhood.

Right there is where we lose people: not only hardened feminists, but any number of decent folk who take satisfaction in contributing to family life through their work, or who suffer from infertility, or have not married for whatever reason and may not find the images conjured up by words like *femininity* and *motherhood* automatically attractive.

To cite a silly example, when I first converted and was eager to "learn the ropes" of my newfound faith, it happened that three of the most faithful Catholic women I knew were much "girlier" than I was or am.

They wore a lot of pink, and any time a faculty member turned up on our university campus with a baby in tow, my friends would squeal and coo and fuss over him as some women will. They seemed moved by an inner prompting not entirely within their control to squeeze and cuddle any child they ever saw. I had no hang-ups about babies, but I did not share this urge myself.

In all the wisdom and experience of my nineteen years (and a few whole months of Catholicism!), I saw all the women around me behave this way and, comparing their effusive affection with my reserved heart, concluded that I wasn't feminine, and wasn't up to motherhood.

I carried this notion that I did not and could not measure up to what the Church expected of me as an unspoken wound in my heart for a long while, until a year spent teaching first-graders in Rome uncovered and developed my rapport with naughty little boys. What a relief to learn I was not a failure as a woman (at the ripe age of twenty-one), but simply had yet to discover my personal way of incarnating the vocation to womanhood.

You're a Genius

When Pope John Paul II issued his 1988 apostolic letter *On the Dignity and Vocation of Women*, he had no intention of advancing a single template of femininity. He was neither shooing moms into the workplace nor sending career women back to their kitchens. He applauded the rise of woman to her rightful place of equal dignity in law and culture, but cautioned that this advance could not bring fulfillment if it came at the expense of her identity as woman, her "feminine genius."

If it's not a love of pastels and a tendency to go doe-eyed over infants, what is the feminine genius exactly? The pope finds it written right into woman's physiology. Even if she never physically carries a child, there is within each woman "room for another" which brings with it innate sensitivity to the goodness of the human person. This sensitivity or power is "spiritual motherhood."

Man, the pope taught, always stands in some sense outside the life process, learning his role as son, husband, and father from woman. Woman, then, has a great service to render humanity as custodian of the person and of the family. She is even entrusted with society at large. In a letter to bishops promulgated by the Congregation for the Doctrine of the Faith in 2004, principal signer Cardinal Joseph Ratzinger — now Pope Benedict XVI — wrote that it is in the family "that the features of a people take shape."[12] Many women contribute to this task physically, as biological mothers, but all women are called to do it spiritually by bringing the truth about the human person to the fore wherever Providence places them.

Spiritual maternity is not a consolation prize for the infertile or those who never marry, even if many women seem to understand *spiritual* in this context, the way my kids would if I offered them spiritual dessert after dinner. Spiritual maternity is real, and it's the inner core that transforms motherhood from a mere biological function into a vocation. Cardinal Ratzinger writes: "It is in not being content only to give physical life that the other truly comes into existence. This means that motherhood can find forms of full realization also where there is no physical procreation."[13]

In stressing the spiritual maternity of all women, the Church is neither imposing physical motherhood on anyone nor forbidding women to have careers. It's simply standing up for women against those who would force them to be just like men (by devaluing motherhood) and those who would reduce them to baby machines (by valuing only physical maternity).

❧❧

If it's not a love of pastels and a tendency to go doe-eyed over infants, what is the feminine genius exactly? Pope John Paul II finds it written right into woman's physiology.

❧❧

Economy Is Women's Work

The human person is designed to love and be loved and cannot find fulfillment outside of what Pope John Paul called "the sincere gift of self"[14] and Pope Benedict calls the "logic of gratuitousness."[15] We're not happy as human beings unless we are giving and receiving love freely. This is especially so for women, because we are designed to be uniquely sensitive to the truth of this reality and to teach it to others.

Nothing could be a more fulfilling object of a woman's creativity, insight, and love, or more important and urgent for humanity, than the nurturing and forming of the next generation. Therefore, Pope John Paul insists, and Pope Benedict reiterates, a woman who desires to dedicate herself full time to being a wife and mother should be permitted to do so without stigma or penalty.

If you're a stay-at-home mom who feels the sting of condescension from people who think you're wasting your life, I'll let you in on a secret most of the world has forgotten. All those people sneering? They work for you.

There was a time when each household had to provide everything for itself. *Economy*, in fact, comes from the Greek word for household management, and it refers to all the activity necessary for a household to have what it needs. Each family planted crops, hunted game, spun its own cloth, and so forth in a division of labor that assured that everyone in the household had what he or she needed to live well. And a household typically included not only a nuclear family, but also extended relatives and servants, because it took a lot of people to perform all the necessary tasks.

"Business" is a form of task specialization by which the household outsources to others what it used to have to do itself. Increasing specialization of this kind has led to massive changes in social organization, but it hasn't changed the essential nature of the activity, which is to provide households with what they need to live well. We don't talk about economics in these terms because we have become philosophical materialists, interested only in *what* and *how*, never concerning ourselves with the questions of origin (Why does this arise?) or purpose (To what end is it ordered?). It's not necessary for a woman to "contribute" to the world of work. The world of work exists to be sure she has what she needs for her family.

Even in strictly material terms, moreover, a woman raising kids at home is performing a great good for society. In *Redeeming Economics*, John Mueller points out that there are two forms of capital. Physical capital, such as production plants, machinery, and computers, which includes all of the items businesses invest in so as to be able to operate. Because businesses employ people and generate wealth, we give them incentives to keep investing in capital. There is also human capital: the minds and muscles of people who design, create, or labor in various businesses. Mueller performs a rough calculation and concludes that two-thirds of wealth creation is a product not of physical, but human, capital. At present we don't incentivize investment in human capital. We don't, for example, provide the same tax breaks for educating a young person that we do for buying a Mac. This means that every adult whom a stay-at-home mom sends into the workforce is an enormous gift of wealth she's given her country.

Raising a family is vitally important work toward which society as a whole is ordered. It does not follow, however, that a fertile married woman should be prohibited from doing anything else, or that work outside the home isn't a legitimate way for a woman to contribute to the good of her household. We need look no further than the Book of Proverbs's idealized description of the good wife to find a woman who is an excellent human resources manager, with a savvy eye for both business and real estate, bringing to the household profit, not loss (see Chapter 31).

The Church's concern is that in the effort to stamp out sex discrimination, women and children are not stamped out in the process; but instead that women's aspirations and the ways they differ from men's are taken into account. Women will harmonize the demands of work and family differently from men. Respect for women means, in the words of Cardinal Ratzinger, that mothers "who wish also to engage in other work should be able to do so with an appropriate work schedule, and not have to choose between relinquishing their family life or enduring continual stress, with negative consequences for one's own equilibrium and the harmony of the family."[16]

There's no Catholic injunction against a woman working outside the home; only the caveat that her work, in order for her to find it fulfilling, must be ordered toward the good of her family and her own person. Presumably Cardinal Ratzinger would approve of innovations such as telecommuting and job-sharing, which are the fruit of women finding ways in which to exercise their skills and serve their families. (Please notice, you ladies who are tempted to think that loving service means running yourself ragged: The Church considers continual stress and the loss of personal equilibrium an unhealthy spiritual condition, not a woman's lot in life. It's not selfish to take care of yourself. It's an investment in harmonious family life.)

You're Needed

Women are not required to abandon work outside the home — far from it. Society needs working women. Pope

John Paul thought that in an increasingly technological and impersonal age, the world would need women to be present in every sector of society to call humanity to itself and defend the goodness of the person against the onslaught of philosophical materialism.

The fact that the pro-life movement and its principal figures are largely women is only the most obvious way we see women at the forefront of defending personhood in public life. I think of my OB-GYN, whose Catholic faith shines as she accompanies patients through the joys and sorrows of the life cycle. She never loses sight of the woman she's treating, even in the midst of dehumanizing tests and procedures. She's given no lectures about it, but her patient-centered practices have spread to colleagues in the hospital where she has privileges. Watching her in action — and the effect that she has on her patients — there can be no doubt that she is doing what she was made to do.

I doubt that "Collette," a clerk at my local grocery, would say she was made to be a cashier, but her Christ-like way of interacting with patrons has made humble work into a genuine apostolate. I have seen regular customers prefer her checkout lane to one with a shorter line simply to bask for a few moments in Collette's smile and words of blessing. Her presence helps make the neighborhood feel like a community. She is bagging groceries, but she is also giving out an experience of Christian kindness — for some, perhaps, the only humanizing, encouraging words they hear all day.

Work Perfects Us

I wonder if you noticed in my account of how I learned to stop worrying and love "the Mom" that a profoundly healing spiritual insight came as a direct fruit of work that I was doing.

That's how work *works*! It is not selfish or materialistic to find joy in the exercise and perfection of skills and talents, or satisfaction in a job well done and the fruits of one's labor. Work is the way the human person participates with God in the fulfillment of creation and the development of his own personality. We don't know what's in us without it.

Few of us, of either sex, have complete liberty to choose exactly what we wish to do with our lives. Even among men, more people have jobs than careers. Our opportunities are limited by our intelligence, personality, economic class, marital status, and plain luck, among other factors. All things being equal, however, our talents, interests, and life experiences tend to reveal to us the way in which we're called to work. If it would be unjust to compel a woman who excels at cooking and sewing to do office work, it's equally unjust to expect a woman who developed a head for business working in her family's print shop to take up knitting out of some arbitrary sense of the feminine.

Trust God More

Perhaps all women — working in or out of the home — would do well to place a little more trust in God, who longs to give us the desires of our hearts.

My son's high school math teacher provides an example. "All I ever wanted to do was teach high school algebra," she told us one back-to-school night. Marriage and the need to make real money intervened, so she worked for a computer company for a time, rising to a high-level position and socking away savings for when the hoped-for children came.

Once they did, she worked part time and then retired from the labor force for a while in order to devote herself to her kids. She was happy and didn't think about algebra.

When her youngest child started high school, however, a college chum invited her to come work for him at our local Catholic high school — teaching algebra!

We spend so much time worrying that we're missing out. Why do we not have more faith that God gives us the grace to do what we must right now? He has a way of working it so that the deepest longings of our hearts find fulfillment in ways we don't expect.

A Life's Work Takes a Lifetime

Generally it is by living our lives today that we gain insight and win grace for tomorrow. Catholics in America are in a hurry, though. "Just tell me what to do, and I'll do it" is our approach to the spiritual life.

This has its merits where faith is concerned. When we receive the sacraments, for example, it's right to trust that if the form has been properly observed, we've indeed received sanctifying grace.

There is no one, holy, catholic, and apostolic lifestyle, however. "Just tell me what to do" is not an authentically Catholic approach to the moral life, because it tries to substitute pat formulas for genuine discernment, patient growth in virtue, and the joy of a deepening relationship with Christ. Christianity is not a complicated set of rules; it's friendship with Jesus.

Your feminine vocation, your motherhood, your life's work, I am arguing, is not bestowed on you like a white silk blouse that comes with elaborate rules for its care. That kind of garment is too delicate for everyday wear — the best you can hope for is not to stain it too obviously.

God's gifts are not like that. He loves us too much.

Your motherhood is more like a seed within you that germinates and sprouts, delicate at first, but growing in time into something sturdy, beautiful, fruitful — and surprising.

Earlier I compared women's work to Christmas in that I don't like the way we think about either. There's a richer comparison to be drawn, though. Mary is the exemplar of Christian womanhood, and what is her role at Christmas? Having discovered her dignity in God, she unites herself to Christ and then bears him to the world in the way God asks of her.

That is the work of every woman.

QUESTIONS FOR REFLECTION

1. It's easy to bemoan negative trends in the culture, but is there any sense in which conditions have improved for Catholic women in your community in the more than two decades since Pope John Paul II wrote On the Dignity and Vocation of Women?

2. It's not uncommon to hear women complain that their work is not appreciated. Is there materialism and envy masked in the complaint?

3. If a space alien had overheard the last three conversations at your Catholic moms' group or some similar gathering, what would he think was most important to Christian women today?

4. *How often am I guilty of rash judgment? Am I quick to think that working women are materialists, that couples with small families must be using contraception, or perhaps that large families are a little weird? How often do I hear remarks like that in my parish or other Catholic community?*

5. *Why do we so easily fall into caricatures of Church teaching on the role of women?*

6. *What is your answer to Régine Pernoud's question: Have we [Christian women] nothing original to propose to the world in our time?*

Rebecca Ryskind Teti is married to Dennis Teti and has four children. She earned an MA in political theory from The Catholic University of America and attended the University of Dallas as an undergrad. Her work has taken various forms, including journalist, pro-life lobbyist, and stay-at-home mom. She currently works at the Center for Family Development in Bethesda, Maryland, and as a chauffeur for her children. She blogs at faithandfamilylive.com.

CHAPTER 7

Fruitful Friendship

By Rachel Balducci

I go through seasons when I could be content to stay in my own little world, putzing around my home and living a life focused on my husband and children. Some days I'm crazy enough to think it's actually easier to be alone.

But that's not true.

When I'm by myself, I'm not growing. Of course, my husband and children are the most important part of my life, but my friends challenge, encourage, and support me in a different way. They fill a unique spot that even the best husband cannot.

Friends keep us sane, make life more fun, and help smooth out the rough edges of our human nature, helping us be the person we were created to be.

Friends Old and New

My closest friend and I have known each other since we were four. I still remember the day we met. My family was moving to a new city on the other side of the state, and though I was sad to leave my grandparents and a host of other relatives, I was young enough to be equally focused on the excitement of our new adventure.

I remember riding in the moving truck next to my dad when we pulled into our new neighborhood. As we drove to the end of a cul-de-sac, I saw a little girl standing in the doorway of the house next door to ours. She would become my bosom friend and partner-in-crime throughout the rest of our childhood.

Her name was Kay. We spent that summer playing in the field that connected our backyards. Our neighborhood didn't have fences, so we had what seemed like miles to explore. In the fall, we started preschool together and remained class-mates from that point until halfway through college, when I moved away for journalism school and Kay studied else-where to become a nurse.

It has now been more than thirty-five years since we met. These days, Kay is a five-minute walk from my house, and between us we have thirteen kids who are themselves the very best of friends.

Over the years our relationship has changed in its breadth and depth. We both married good men who have become our best friends in that unique way that a good hus-band does. And we have sisters who weren't even born when Kay and I met but who now hold a special place in our lives, who lend a listening ear and supportive voice as sisters do.

But the truth is, this friend of mine is as close to being a sister as you can be, short of being from the same mom and dad. The relationship flows from years of mutual respect and love — of being there together in good times and bad and, mostly, of just really liking each other.

Having a lifelong friend is a luxury, and I'm richly blessed. I also have a core group of friends I've known almost my entire life, and I've made new friends within the past few years. It's nice to know I can still do that in the midst of this very busy season of life.

I'm aware of how difficult it can be to connect with good people, however. Not everyone can (or should be) a friend. As I reflect on my friendships, I realize that they have three key elements.

My friends and I:

- Have a common interest. Jesus and life in him are the primary interests I share with most of my friends. The underlying current in these relationships—and it's not all that underlying — is that everything we discuss and revel in has a bottom-line goal: to draw us closer to Christ.

- We still have a good time — we're not constantly immersed in spiritual conversation — but we support each other in our quest to follow Christ while living out the teachings of the Church. Not all of my friends fall into this category — they're not all Christians — but those friends can't speak to the heart of issues in the same way.

- Trust each other. Not everyone is comfortable sharing from the heart. That's okay. But in order to make deep friendships, you have to be willing to be honest. My closest friends are women with whom I can be totally and utterly myself. They bring out the best in me, and I do that for them.

- Are on the same wavelength. I have lots of friends, but I jive a little better with some more than others. That doesn't make the others less special, just a little different.

It helps to understand that certain relationships are set apart because the friends are on the same wavelength. Don't expect to connect with every person in the same way.

❦

"A faithful friend is a sturdy shelter; he who finds one finds a treasure." — Sirach 6:14 (NAB)

❦

How to Make Friends

When I was a girl and feeling sad or wishing someone would invite me over, my mom would turn the tables and tell me to do the inviting. If I complained that no one ever called me, she'd direct me to the contraption on the wall and suggest I phone a friend.

She was right, and I continue to remind myself of her advice because, in spite of my friendships, there are days when I sit back and feel sorry for myself. I watch the phone and lament that no one has called. I wonder why no one has sent me a witty, encouraging text. I look out the window and see two friends out for a fitness walk and wonder why no one got in touch with me.

And then I ask myself, "Who have you called today?" It's very easy to sit back and wonder why-oh-why no one is trying to be my friend without considering what I myself have done to reach out to others. If I want to get together for lunch, no one will know that unless I make the effort to arrange it.

If you want to have a friend, be a friend.

Making new friends can be intimidating and scary, but it's absolutely worth the effort. We need friends to help us be who God wants us to be.

Here are some practical tips for making new friends:

- Open your eyes. Take advantage of opportunities to meet people — in the church cry room, at the preschool open house, at the gym, and in similar settings.

- Don't be afraid to ask. Call a neighbor and invite her over for coffee. Invite a family over for dinner, even if your house isn't picture perfect. They won't notice. Don't be shy — make the effort!

- When someone asks you to get together — say yes! Maybe you're an introvert; maybe you're too tired; maybe you feel awkward. It doesn't matter. Unless you have a compelling reason for avoiding a situation, you should try to respond positively to friendly overtures from other people.

- Get out of your comfort zone and away from your to-do list. Don't let an over-scheduled calendar prevent you from making friends.

"Friendship is born at that moment when one person says to another: What! You too? I thought I was the only one."[17]

— C.S. Lewis

Good Friends Are for Each Other

I appreciate it when people call and offer comfort when things are tough. I value words of encouragement and expressions of sympathy. It means a lot when people go out of their way to say they care and that they are praying for me when I'm struggling.

What means even more to me is friends who rejoice with me when things are going well — who are there for me to show support in my shining moments. This can be hard for some people — I think especially for women. We sometimes get caught up in a competitiveness that can be deadly for friendships.

We don't need to always be focusing on other people's victories, but in a healthy friendship there must be an ability to wholeheartedly and without reserve rejoice in someone else's win. As my mom always told me growing up (and sometimes reminds me to this day!): "Someone else's win is not your loss."

Good friends build each other up; they don't bring each other down.

Allow Yourself to Be Vulnerable

St. Frances of Rome came from a wealthy family, and although she wanted to be a nun, she accepted the marriage her parents had arranged for her with the son of an equally wealthy family. She gave herself generously to the marriage, but mourned the lost opportunity to serve Jesus in the poor and to live a simple life. Her sister-in-law,

Vanozza, found her sobbing one day and, in a moment of vulnerability, revealed that she, too, yearned for a humble life of faith and service.

This was a pivotal moment for Frances who, with Vanozza, then found the courage to practice holiness in an environment neither would have chosen. Because Vanozza risked opening herself up — risked being a friend — Frances found new strength and eventually went on to become a great saint.

Isn't this how good friendships work? A heart-to-heart conversation, trust, vulnerability — these help us cut to the heart of our struggles and laugh in the face of frustration and adversity.

Good Friends Can Be Trusted with Our Vulnerability

I've had friendships in which I've had to keep my cards close to my chest. That's okay, I guess, but there was something about those relationships that left me feeling a little depleted. For whatever reason, I couldn't be totally honest about my struggles, my ups and downs, and even my victories. (I didn't want to sound like I was bragging.)

Perhaps part of the problem was that those women themselves were not willing to share on a deeper level. We don't need to walk around wearing our heart on our sleeve with everyone, but we can only be truly close to those who are willing to be as totally honest with us as we are with them. If I'm inclined to think your life is perfect, for example, and if you are inclined to make it look that way, it's going to be hard for me to show my weakness. It's a vicious cycle.

This means that you will not be close with everyone you meet, but if you want to have close, healthy friendships, be prepared to get real.

The Strained Friendship

My spiritual director and I once discussed my frustration with a relationship that just didn't feel as true as it could be. Despite what I thought were untold efforts on my part, I felt a strain in the friendship — and a sadness.

"Is it realistic that I can somehow make this better?" I asked.

"No," he finally said. This is an imperfect world, he explained, and even with our best intentions and total reliance on Jesus, there will still be relationships that feel strained. We are not in heaven … not yet.

This was hard to hear. I want so badly to believe that if I try hard enough I can break through whatever barriers hold someone back in a friendship. But the truth is that for whatever reason, we might not bring out the best in everyone, and vice versa. Maybe it's our wounds holding us back; maybe it's theirs. Regardless, from time to time we'll encounter that friend who makes us cling to the foot of the cross in order to get through.

Even the saints struggled with this. St. Thérèse of Lisieux was very honest about her struggle with a fellow nun. Thérèse sometimes went out of her way to spend time with that woman, because those interactions made her that much more dependent on Jesus.

That's not to say that we need to live with conflict and consternation — if we've offended someone to the point of wrongdoing, we should fix that — but some friendships will be difficult and require a measure of self-sacrifice on our part.

Toxic Friendships

There is room in life for lots of friends: a few very intimate, heart-on-sleeve friendships; a few more here's-how-I'm-really-doing friends; and many of the solid we-enjoy-time-together friendships.

But what there is not room for in life is a toxic friendship.

Toxic friendships sometimes involve lots of crying or bellyaching. This is not to say that you can't ever listen to a friend complain, or that if a friend calls you crying you should hang up. In fact, an important part of friendship is listening and offering strong support.

But if that's what it's always about, then the friendship has become toxic, and it's time to step away.

If someone frequently calls you in tears or to unload the latest drama, she's not being a good friend. You need to take a breather, at least until the situation brightens. That's not being a fair-weather friend. That's being smart and setting good boundaries. You might not need to step away entirely, but you might need to limit your time with that person.

If you find yourself in a toxic relationship, here are some charitable ways to set boundaries.

- ◆ Don't immediately amputate the relationship. Give the person a chance. Once you've noticed things are toxic, make a decision that during the next phone call or encounter, you will limit the time you spend listening to a vent.

- ◆ Once you've reached that limit, change the subject. Steer things in a more positive direction. This gives your friendship the opportunity to exist outside the negativity and gives you the chance to see whether you can continue in this relationship — in this season — without getting caught up in drama.

♦ If that doesn't work and the person insists on continuing the complaining and negativity, limit the phone calls you take and the time you are together. This isn't rude or unkind; it's creating healthy limits, both for yourself and your friend.

When a friendship isn't in good working order, it's not doing what it's meant to do — strengthen us, support us, draw us closer to Jesus. It's time to give yourself some space.

And remember: This works both ways — you don't want to be a toxic friend to someone else!

For instance, during one uniquely challenging season in my life, I realized that all I wanted to do when talking to friends was complain and analyze. I was unhappy with certain details of my life, but I finally realized that all my talking and navel-gazing was making me a drag. It was time to change those circumstances — or my attitude — and get back to a better place emotionally.

To Mend or Not to Mend

Aside from overly negative interactions, there can be tough seasons in the healthiest of friendships: misunderstandings, words said that should not have been, feelings inadvertently hurt. A relationship with a significant history and a deep investment of time and emotion is a relationship worth fighting for.

In my healthiest friendships, there have been times when I picked up a vibe (or sent a vibe!), and wrongdoing had to be repaired. Being the wrong*doer* isn't fun, and we all know the struggle involved in apologizing and repairing that hurt.

Dealing properly with *being wronged*, though, going to a friend to admit that something they said or did really hurt my feelings, is a special kind of struggle. I have learned that it's worth feeling a little bit embarrassed to admit a hurt and deal with it — get it in the light — rather than trying to figure out how to forget something that was painful.

Not only can a good friendship handle this, but it will be stronger for it.

Then, sadly, there are those friendships that can't be fixed, wounds and misunderstandings that can't be healed, maybe because the measures needed for healing are too much for the relationship to bear. Perhaps one or both friends are unwilling to be honest about their feelings. Not everyone is comfortable admitting that they have been hurt. Not everyone is willing to admit that they have been wrong. In these situations you do the best you can do to address any wrongdoing and then leave it at that.

The key is to approach every friend with humility and love. This doesn't mean being a doormat or pretending you're not hurt if you are. It does mean being willing to see things from the other's point of view and to be loving when dealing with differences in personality and opinion.

Good Friends Cheer You Up

My friend Susie and I have known each other since we were eight. Here's the thing I love about Susie: she always cheers me up. Not because she tells me I'm crazy (though she sometimes does), but because she rarely makes me *feel* like I'm crazy. She always empathizes — in a way that doesn't patronize me, but somehow lets me know that I'm not alone.

Susie and I had a season, not too long ago, when we found ourselves with small children again after a few years without. Getting back into the groove of having a baby was a challenge; but even bigger challenges came a year later when Susie was having another baby, and then the next year, when I was too.

It was an intense time for both of us, and we would take turns talking each other down from our crazy. Some days I would call her, fighting back tears, and sometimes the tables were turned. Some days I didn't even try to hide the tears, and I sobbed on the phone like the big, overwhelmed baby that I was.

In our darkest, most stressed-out moment, Susie and I once plotted to get an apartment together in which to hang out on the weekends. We reasoned that our husbands would do a great job of taking care of the kids (they totally would), and we could use our new pad to catch our breath and get a sanity check.

Instead, we opted to go grab a few large margaritas at the local Mexican place. We felt much better about life in general after that. We decided we'd go home after all.

A good friend is someone to whom you can pour out your heart and trust that they will talk you back from the edge. A good friend will let you talk until you're talked out and then say, "Okay, where are you going to go from here?"

What you don't want in a friend is a session of whining that goes nowhere. That doesn't help you in your quest to be a good Catholic. A good friend listens to what you're saying and then maybe offers advice — and in your darkest hour is never afraid to do just that. Then she encourages you. She might tell you that you are perfectly justified in your fatigue or frustration or sadness or ennui, but she will never, ever encourage you in your selfishness.

The Heart of Every Good Friendship

A few years ago, Henry, our youngest son, broke his leg. Thanks to a crazy set of unpredictable circumstances, our dog managed to whip the toddler into the air so that when he landed, he split his femur.

That accident led to seven weeks in a full body cast for Henry. It was one of my most challenging mothering experiences to date.

At some point in those weeks, we were desperate to get out of the house. I needed to buy groceries and find some new entertainment for Henry.

To my dismay, I was unable to go by myself. Henry needed to be pushed in a stroller that had a crazy home-rigged system for keeping his cast where it needed to be. The things I needed at the store required a cart and thus a second set of hands. I needed help.

So I called a friend who assured me that she was more than happy to pitch in. In fact, she was honored that I asked.

We spent the morning at the store, Henry and I, my friend and her son. We even stopped for coffee on the way. It was one of the most memorable and relaxing moments in that very hard and seemingly endless season.

I needed my friend, and she was willing to help. And it blessed us both.

Sometimes friendships are strengthened by our ability to reach out, to admit that we need others and that we can't go it alone.

That, to me, is at the heart of every good friendship: admitting that this person fills a void in your life, that she is Jesus to you in moments of weakness and of strength. For all of us, being a good friend means being the hands and feet of Jesus not just in those moments when we serve one another without counting the cost, but also in the moments when we laugh until we cry or share what is in the deepest, most tender places of our heart.

QUESTIONS FOR REFLECTION

1. Am I able to make good friends? If not, what is holding me back from making the connections that would allow me to support and encourage others and let them support and encourage me?

2. What qualities do I look for in a friend? Which of these will help me form strong and lasting friendships? Am I spending time with people who draw me closer to Christ?

3. Do I have toxic friendships in my life? Do I allow others to dump on me or spend time complaining about their own problems? Do I have a healthy balance between being a good listener and knowing when to end a conversation?

4. How do I handle conflict with friends? When someone offends me, am I comfortable with telling them?

5. *Am I willing to be vulnerable with those I really trust? If not, what is holding me back?*

6. *Do I have someone in my life I can call in a moment of crisis — someone who will listen to me, and then encourage me in my challenges? If not, how can I find such a friend? How can I be a friend like that to others in my life?*

Rachel Balducci is married to Paul, and they have five boys and one sweet girl. Rachel is the author of *How Do You Tuck In a Superhero?* and writes a weekly column for *The Southern Cross*, the newspaper for the Diocese of Savannah. She maintains her personal blog Testosterhome at http://testosterhome.net, where she muses about life and staying sane in a house filled with males.

CHAPTER 8

We Said Yes

Danielle Bean

I can't write the marriage chapter. I have no business writing the marriage chapter.

My husband and I are just coming off a twenty-four-hour stint of avoiding eye contact and communicating through the children because ... well, I kind of forget why. Something about whose job it was to pay the phone bill that didn't get paid. And he was such a jerk, you would not have believed it. Really, he was, I'm sure you understand.

In the throes of this recent cold war, I texted a complaint to a friend.

"Is it really so terrible of me to notice and care that I am *always* the one who tries to make up first after a fight?"

"I've done that," she replied. "It gets pretty lonely up there on that hill with only your principles to keep you warm."

Figures she'd go and get all reasonable on me. Not ready to grow up and quit complaining just yet, I called my sister instead.

Do you see what I mean? I have no business writing the marriage chapter.

Hard and Fast

Dan and I were kids when we got married seventeen years ago. I was the only female in my college class to graduate while wearing an engagement ring.

Fall in love, hurry up and get married? People simply didn't do that kind of thing anymore. One of my professors even advised that I not wear my engagement ring on job interviews because prospective employers might wonder about the priorities of a woman who was hellbent on getting married so young.

They would have been right to wonder. I graduated in May, secured a job in June, got married in July, and birthed our honeymoon baby nine months later.

I look at our wedding photos now and laugh out loud at our wide-eyed innocence. We look about eleven years old. And deliriously happy.

Of course we were happy. We had no idea what we were getting ourselves into. We knew only that whatever lay ahead, we were in it together. Forever. For good. We just had no way of knowing the kind of pain and sacrifice those kinds of words might require.

In the years following our wedding day, we grew up hard and fast, together.

And now, just in case "growing up hard and fast, together" sounds even remotely romantic, let me assure you that though there might be some sweetness in hindsight, the day-to-day grind of living out life in the trenches of a young marriage with a fast-growing family are not very romantic at all.

There was morning sickness. And colicky infants. And sleepless nights. And bills that piled up faster than our paychecks did.

We had energy, optimism, and babies. In spades. But those things only get you so far when the phone bill needs paying.

Dan and I have always loved the movie *It's a Wonderful Life*. We watch it together every year on Christmas Eve while getting ready for Midnight Mass. One of my favorite lines comes when George Bailey and his guardian angel, Clarence, discuss the $8,000 that George needs to cover his deficit at the bank.

Clarence has no money, he explains, because they have no need for such things in heaven. But it's George Bailey's response that rings true:

"Well, it comes in pretty handy down here, Bub!"

Indeed it does. Worldly needs are real, and they can be such a distraction from our heavenly ideals.

And speaking of heavenly ideals, I am going to step out for just a moment here to tell my husband that I'm sorry about the phone-bill thing. And maybe make him a nice lunch or something. Then I'll be able to write the rest of this chapter — especially the sacrificial love parts — with some measure of credibility.

On This Rock

One day a few years ago, two-year-old Daniel jabbed a small, pudgy finger at my face in the wedding photo.

"Mama," he announced confidently; and then, "Papa," as he pointed to his father.

"Yes," I told him. "That's Mama and Papa on the day we were married."

He squinted at the photo for another moment before turning to me with an earnest question.

"Where's Danny?"

So began a conversation in which I told him for the first time about his beginnings. For the first time, this small boy attempted an understanding of the world that existed before he was.

Some of my older kids have coined a phrase for the time "before you were born."

"You wouldn't remember that," I hear them tell younger siblings, "because back then you were No Such Thing."

No Such Thing. It sounds terribly sad; and yet, by contrast, what a lovely idea for each of them to realize that one day they did indeed become Some Thing. That day, when I told Daniel that God made him, saw that he was good, and placed him inside of me to grow, his brown eyes glowed. When I told him that he stretched and moved and grew until at last he was big enough to come out of the darkness and meet us, he beamed. When I described what a joy it was for us to see him, hold him, and kiss him at last, he wriggled with delight.

Rooted in Love

Every child likes to know how he began. And he especially likes to know that his beginnings were rooted in love.

Five-year-old Gabrielle has a budding interest in the subject of love. When it comes to romance, she is the giggling girl of a thousand questions.

"How did you know you and Papa were in love?" she asks with shining eyes. "Did he get hearts in his eyes when he looked at you, like what happens in cartoons?"

And then she waits, breathless in anticipation of the wonders I am about to describe. So far, my descriptions of two awkward teenagers holding hands with sweaty palms, writing long letters, and talking on the phone for hours on end have not disappointed.

One of Gabrielle's favorite objects is a small rock that is covered with worn pink paint, tiny red hearts, and the words "I love you."

She never tires of looking at and asking me about this gift that I made and gave to her father almost twenty years ago. When I tell her how her father used to work late at night and I would stay up, waiting for his phone calls and doing things like painting and writing to keep myself busy, she turns the rock over in her hand and smiles with wonder.

Back then, Gabby might have been No Such Thing, but the love that would make us a family was already there.

For me, the "I Love You" rock is a reminder of the sturdy foundation our marriage is meant to be for our family. Dan and I might not spend much time painting love notes on rocks these days, but we still do love. It's just a different kind of love that expresses itself in a different kind of way.

As intoxicating as romance feels in the beginning of a relationship, as happy as an in-love couple can be when they are focused only on each other, ultimately, God means for them to give themselves to greater things.

Back when I had time for rock painting, I might have had an inkling of what our "greater things" might be, but I did not yet know their names. They surround us today — all eight of them — playing, laughing, crying, spilling, shouting, fighting, and making all manner of joyful noise. They groan and roll their eyes when they see me wrap my arms around their father's neck in the kitchen and plant a lipstick kiss on his cheek.

And yet they see security in that kiss. They see their roots and their beginnings. They see the love that allowed them to be. I know what they see, because, though they roll their eyes, they smile, too.

〰〰

As intoxicating as romance feels in the beginning of a relationship, as happy as an in-love couple can be when they are focused only on each other, ultimately, God means for them to give themselves to greater things.

〰〰

Till Death Do We Part

It's not always painted rocks and kisses, though, is it? I already told you about the stupid phone-bill fight, but we've had tougher times than that. I'd like to say I have always handled the tough times as a model of maturity, leaning hard on the graces that God gives us in the sacrament of marriage. But I'd also like to not be a liar.

Dan and I have had our share of unhappy times. Times when we both felt distant. Tired. Unloved. And unloving. Times when I think, if ever we had allowed the word to be a part of our vocabulary, we would have said — or at least thought — of divorce.

I think every couple has times like that, but our Church is wise enough to teach us that marriage is forever. For those of us committed to remaining faithful to Catholic teaching, that leaves us one option: lump it. But if lumping it gets old, you might try putting some effort into repairing your relationship.

〰️〰️

I'd like to say I have always handled the tough times as a model of maturity, leaning hard on the graces God gives us in the sacrament of marriage. But I'd also like to not be a liar.

〰️〰️

Take Care of Him

A woman I do not know once sent me a very personal plea. It happens on the Internet. Perfect strangers share instant intimacy.

"Help me love my husband better," she wrote in an email. "I want to love him, but it's so hard some days."

I know how hard it is, but here is what I wrote to her anyway:

"I do not know the details of what is going on in your marriage, so I can't speak about specifics, but perhaps that is just as well. I think that maybe the most valuable thing I can offer you, or any woman who struggles with her husband, is a bit of generalized advice.

"Take care of him."

It sounds simplistic, but the most important thing any woman can do for the health of her marriage, her family, and, ultimately, herself is to take care of her husband.

Taking care of him means first of all not demeaning him. Some women refer to their husbands as another child to care for, but do your kids work jobs and pay the bills? Do your kids change the oil in your car and keep your health insurance premiums paid? Did your kids vow before God to love you for richer or for poorer, in sickness and in health, for better or for worse, till death do you part?

It's socially acceptable to mock men and demean dads. Commercials and sitcoms portray the father characters as buffoons and the women as their moral superiors. Real marriages, however, are made up of two flawed human beings trying, and sometimes failing, to love and serve one another.

Did I say *serve*?

Why, yes I did. I've said this before and gotten a bit of flak for it, but why should it be controversial to suggest that wives take care of their husbands? How did we women become so twisted in our thinking that many of us consider the idea of doing nice things for someone we have vowed to love forever as somehow absurd? How is it demeaning or beneath us to take care of someone we profess to love?

Take care of him.

You know your husband better than anyone else, and you know what's important to him. No matter what else is going on in your marriage (exceptions made, of course, for abusive situations or mental illness), you cannot help but improve your marriage by taking care of your husband.

Yes, it can be hard. That is why we need the graces of a sacrament to do these simple yet heroic things: make his favorite foods; make sure his laundry is caught up; ask him about his work; notice and thank him for all his contributions; make an effort to spend time alone with him on a regular basis. He's not a monster, this man you married. He can't help but respond positively and look for ways to be your hero when he sees and feels your heroic, heartfelt love and devotion.

If you don't feel up to it, remind yourself of the many ways he serves you and your family. For example, Dan's contributions to our family life came into sharp focus for me the other night while listening to the sound of smoke alarms beeping in the house.

There was no need to evacuate. You see, our smoke detectors are wired electrically, but they have backup batteries. When the backup batteries get old or begin to run low, the detectors do this really handy thing — they beep to remind you. All of them at once. Every 18 seconds. Usually beginning at 2:30 in the morning.

That night, as I lay partially awake discovering this fact and reveling in the convenience of it all, I heard a thump at the end of my bed. I opened my eyes and saw my husband standing there with a ladder. He spent the next ten minutes balanced precariously on the ladder, fumbling with a screwdriver in the dark and replacing the batteries. Then he moved on to the next smoke detector, and then the next one, until at last the house was quiet again.

When he returned to bed, I might have mumbled a thank you, but there was no thunderous applause. No band played. There were no high-fives. This was just an everyday dad doing what everyday dads do: whatever needs doing. In the middle of the night, and with no expectation that anyone will even be awake enough to thank him for it.

My hero.

Five Ways to Love Your Man

If work stress, job loss, or some other challenge has your man down these days, you, his wife — the one he looks to most for love and affirmation — are in a unique position to help him feel like a hero again.

Here are some practical ways we wives can build up our husbands during difficult times:

1. Hear him. Sometimes your husband just wants to express his thoughts and feelings to a nonjudgmental listener. If he vents about difficult people in his office, the evil boss who laid him off, or the lousy weather, let him do it.

   Keep in mind, though, that men communicate more directly than women. Don't interrupt with your own observations or "listen" while you change the baby's diaper and sweep the floor. Your man will feel loved if you maintain eye contact and do nothing else while he speaks.

2. Feed him. Food might not be the only way to a man's heart, but it surely is an effective one. Is there a recipe your husband enjoys that you haven't made in awhile? Find time to make it this week. Is there a dish he always orders at a nearby restaurant? Get it to go and surprise him with it tonight.

   It's not so much the food itself as it is the thought behind it that will make your husband feel loved. You can make sure he has a hot breakfast, bring him a beer, or simply set the table and light some candles to make ordinary fare more enticing.

3. Touch him. It can be difficult for us women to understand sometimes, but sex really is the primary way most men communicate love. If his ego has been bruised, initiating intimacy or being a little flirtatious is a sure way to make him feel like the powerful, attractive man you know he is. Give him an unexpected kiss, offer a back rub, or send an email to let him know you're thinking about him and can't wait to spend time alone with him.

4. Serve him. What are some little things you can do to make your husband feel cared for? You might declutter a spot in the house where he likes to unwind, fill his drawer with clean socks and underwear, make sure the shower has a fresh bar of soap before his shower, or take out the trash without saying a word. His life is rough right now. These small acts of service will smooth some of the rough edges and help him relax.

5. Pray. Ask God to shower him with grace. You might also think of some small cross you regularly endure — carpools, folding laundry, dealing with tantrums — and offer it up for your husband's intentions. That way, when these small sacrifices present themselves, you will not only have something to offer up for your husband but a built-in reminder to pray for him as well.

If all else fails, show him this list and ask for his input. Tell him how much you want to support him, and ask him how you can best do that. Just knowing that you are in his corner might be exactly the kind of encouragement he needs.

He Said, She Said

Now, all this husband-loving stuff is great, you might be thinking, but what about when your man is being a jerk? I mean *really a jerk?* You know that he is sometimes.

Of course I know that. You don't survive seventeen years of marriage without realizing this. And, oh yeah, you're a jerk sometimes, too.

Other times, though, neither of you is being a jerk. The two of you are victims of misunderstanding and miscommunication. Eve ate the apple, and Adam did, too. So here we are.

Let me give you an example. It all started with an innocent comment. An innocent comment made by a loving husband to his devoted wife. As any married person knows, however, communication between the sexes can be tricky business. And by tricky, I mean absolutely, irrefutably impossible. Here is what happened.

We were on our way home from Mass one Sunday morning when my dear husband turned to me and said, "You should get your hair done."

Now, Dan is a man. Like most men, his usual mode of communication is a kind of foreign language I call man-talk. I had no idea at the time, but apparently in man-talk, "You should get your hair done," means something akin to, "I love you, and I know looking nice is important to you. You work so hard, and you never think about yourself — you deserve to take a little break to have your hair done. I'll gladly watch the kids. Why don't you make an appointment this week sometime?"

I should have realized that. But then I am a woman and specialize in an entirely different dialect — woman-talk. In woman-talk, "You should get your hair done," loosely translates into, "You look so old and frumpy that I am embarrassed to be seen in public with you. Fix yourself up, would ya?"

I was insulted. And hurt. And deeply offended. Regrettably, I responded to my husband's apparent unkindness as a wounded woman. "Well, if I ever had a minute to myself, maybe I could give some thought to my hair!" I barked in his direction before assuming the defensive posture of arms folded across my chest and lower lip protruding outward.

Anyone fluent in woman-talk would have known that by my snippy retort I simply meant, "Your opinion matters a great deal to me, and it hurts to think that you might not like my hairstyle. I would love to make an appointment at the hair salon, but I don't want to impose on your free time by leaving you alone with the children."

But Dan is not a woman, and because of the inevitable language barrier that implies, he could not guess at the true meaning behind my words. He stared at me in stunned silence, wondering at my resentful response to what he thought was a loving suggestion.

I'll spare you all of the embarrassing details, but as usually happens in marital miscommunication, things spiraled downward from there.

This man-talk/woman-talk thing is one of the differences between men and women. Before I was married, I knew that it was because we are so different that men and women are capable of working so well together. What I did not know, however, is that it is because of those same differences that men and women are capable of driving one another crazy.

St. Augustine once said, "This is the very perfection of a man, to find out his own imperfections." Well, there is nothing quite like married life to bring one's own imperfections and shortcomings to light. Part of the beauty of the vocation of marriage, though, is that you can get a little bit better at it, a little bit at a time, with a whole lot of practice every day. It's a calling that is rich with built-in rewards and unexpected blessings.

In fact, at the end of that miserable Sunday of our colossal misunderstanding, Dan brought home a small package of M&Ms and presented them to me as a peace offering. I'm still working on man-talk, and he still struggles with woman-talk, but happily for both of us, chocolate means love. In any language.

Five Ways to Build Your Marriage

Sharing a household and raising a family with someone who is so different from ourselves challenges us to strengthen our marriage and sacrifice for the good of the one we love. Here are some practical tips to help us do that.

1. **Make time for each other.**
    Busy family life and work schedules will never leave wide-open spaces in which to connect with your husband. Make spending time together a priority, and then make the time for it. Your married "dates" don't all have to be fancy dinners out, though. You can schedule time for coffee together in the morning, open a bottle of wine after the kids have gone to bed, or watch a movie on a lazy weekend afternoon. Just spend that time together.

2. **Say "I love you."**
    I've heard some wives complain that saying "I love you" all the time when leaving each other or ending a phone call

can become routine and therefore (they think) meaningless. I think that saying "I love you" *should* be routine. It can be said in more meaningful moments, too, of course, but committed love is supposed to be a routine part of your married relationship. Make it a habit! Say it often!

3. **Do things together.**

Nothing builds a marriage like shared goals. I hope that you and your spouse already share long-term goals like getting to heaven and the well-being of your children, but short-term goals are also important parts of building a healthy marriage. Plan a household project together, cook a meal together, or set fitness goals you can share. Bonding is made of small stuff like this!

4. **Apologize.**

"I'm sorry" are some of the most healing words you can ever speak in your marriage. It's easy for a man and woman who live together in a committed relationship to take each other for granted and hurt each other's feelings with thoughtless words and actions. If you've been fighting, even if your spouse shares some of the blame, never hesitate to say "I'm sorry" and work toward reconciliation. The sooner, the better.

5. **Pray.**

As in the tips for loving your man, prayer is essential to strengthening your bond. Pray for your marriage during your own prayer time, but also pray with your spouse if he is willing. Ask God to bless your relationship with the graces you gained in the Sacrament of Matrimony. Pray to your spouse's guardian angel, asking for protection and to draw closer to Christ.

Feel the Music

These days, when songs from the eighties come on the radio, I sometimes want to turn them up and tell my kids to listen carefully. After all, they have a right to know where they come from. This is the music, I want to tell them, that played while I sat in the vinyl seats of your father's maroon, hand-me-down Chevy Celebrity while wearing high-top Reebok sneakers and the finest pair of stonewashed jeans.

It's the music that played as we cruised back roads and talked about the important stuff — like how we can know that God exists, and how many kids we might have, and whether or not we were too cool to go to the prom. It's the music that played when we made childish mistakes, fell in love too hard too soon, and wound up fighting and separating but never really giving up the notion that God had a plan for the two of us.

We just didn't know yet what that plan would be.

Back then, there was no email, I tell my wide-eyed children. Your father used to mail me handwritten letters, and he would draw tiny pencil sketches on the outside of the envelopes.

Didn't you know that your father could draw?

My favorite illustration was that of a young couple sitting outside on a blanket, leaning against the thick trunk of a leafy oak tree. A short way off, in the distance, a small child toddled in the grass. The child was a miniature figure — no more than a tiny triangle with stick legs and outstretched bits of arms, but that tiny figure was a shade of a dream. That small shadow of a child was a representation of something big we felt God was calling us toward — and yet something we knew nothing about.

But we said *yes,* because the attractive force of even the vague idea of marriage, of parenthood, of together forever was too unknown and yet too strangely wonderful to refuse.

Recently, Dan sat working at the computer while a throng of children wandered in and out, between rooms and around his legs, in his lap, and on the desk in front of him.

He clicked a familiar song in my iTunes account and announced: "Listen up, kids. This one is dedicated to your mother."

That's right, I thought, as the music surrounded me and the undone dishes, the unfolded laundry, and the clingy baby in my arms. Listen up, kids. Because we said *yes.* To you, and to all your brothers and sisters. Without knowing about the colic and the tantrums, the morning sickness and the financial fear, we said *yes.* Without knowing about the 3 a.m. vomit and the heartbreak that comes from loving so hard, and yet knowing that it cannot possibly be returned, we said *yes.*

But what we also didn't know was that the tiny toddler who wandered through the sketches of grass so long ago would come and steal our hearts eight times over. We didn't know that the child would teach us to love and to give in ways we never before thought possible. We didn't know how big God was.

But now perhaps we do. Just a little bit, we do.

QUESTIONS FOR REFLECTION

1. Do you see your marriage as "the rock" on which your family is built? What are some things that distract and confuse you when it comes to treating your marriage as the primary relationship that it is, and how can you overcome these?

2. Do you struggle with the idea of "taking care" of your husband? What gets in the way? Pride? Past hurts? A sense of injustice? What specific attitudes and feelings stand in the way of showing your spouse more tender love beginning right now, and what can you do to change them?

3. Who has a marriage that you admire? Consider the actions and qualities of the woman in that relationship and list three specific ways you can emulate those qualities in your own marriage.

4. Is your husband your hero? Think of a time when he impressed you with the strength of his love and describe that moment in detail.

5. Do you pray for your marriage? What specific marital graces do you need to ask Jesus for right now?

6. In what ways is your husband different from you? What gifts does he have that you don't share? Note the ways in which these differences intrigue and attract you, and the ways in which they drive you crazy. What might help you remember to look at his differences as a gift?

Danielle Bean is a wife, mother of eight, and editor-in-chief of *Catholic Digest*.

CHAPTER 9

Receiving, Creating, and Letting Go: Motherhood in Body and Soul

Simcha Fisher

I have nine kids. You may think that's why I'm writing the chapter on motherhood — because I'm such an expert. It's true   just as the kid who had to keep repeating third grade is an expert on third grade. Some people just need extra time to get the basics down. Nine children in, I think I'm starting to get the hang of this motherhood thing.

Why is it so hard? Can there really be anything special about motherhood, since it's so, well, *common*? Why is there even anything to say, when becoming a mother is something that can happen in an instant, to the experts and the ignorant, the desperate and the unwilling, the fearful and the overconfident—and when women who long for motherhood sometimes find themselves bereft?

How is it that Eve, who had no idea what she was getting into, has anything in common with Mary, who was already more prepared when she was conceived than the rest of us are in our prime?

And what do these two women have in common with us?

You may not like the answer. You may find it insulting, or incomplete, or just weird. But I am convinced that when we physically become mothers, our bodies tell the story of what God wants our souls to do. When we conceive, gestate, and give birth, we are doing what all women are called to do whether they raise twenty children or none: *to be receptive, to be creative, and then, when the time is right, to let go.*

A tall order, with subtle implications. Our Lady is the ultimate role model for mothers, but how helpful can she really be to us in the trenches? She only had one child, after all! And she didn't have to deal with original sin. Another puzzle: How is it that the holiest woman I know is also the most motherly, but has no children at all?

Mary and my childless friend both point to the same idea: motherhood is about more than the physical. All women are called to a spiritual motherhood that extends beyond bearing and caring for biological children. Mary modeled this vocation in spades, as mother of us all. Childless holy women follow their vocation in a less obvious but perhaps more admirable way, without the guide of the body to train their souls.

Some women find comfort and direction in the concept of spiritual motherhood; others bristle at the phrase, hearing in it a condescending "consolation prize" of an idea.

I can only tell you what I know. So this chapter is about what I have learned from conceiving, carrying, and bearing children, and what that's taught me about the vocation of women. Some of these ideas don't have to do with children at all; and some apply equally to children and to everyone else a woman encounters.

That is the job that women have, whether we have ever given birth or not: to be a mother to the whole world. God knows the whole world needs us.

❦❦

**That is the job that women have,
whether we have ever given birth or not:
to be a mother to the whole world.
God knows the whole world needs us.**

❦❦

A Mother Is Receptive

O modern woman, does the idea of receptivity make you a little itchy? You're all in favor of the motherly virtues of strength and wisdom, good council and courage — all very valiant, very Joan of Arc. But receptivity? Isn't that kind of ... passive? Don't you just imagine a reclining reed of a woman, her tentative profile framed in lace, trembling among the potted ferns as she waits for Life to happen to her?

I know, that's not you. Even if such an image appeals to your romantic side, a soft fantasy like this comes rapidly un-stuffed the first time you're up all night wrestling among milky sheets with a baby who is as hungry as three frantic wolves, but somehow can't figure out, after all this time, *how to find the nipple*. And when the sun rises on your sleepless face, you're *still supposed to get up and do stuff*. "Poof" go the last feathery rags of that gentle mist of motherhood, and "Howdy!" barks the harsh, daylight reality of your new life as Mom.

In truth, there is very little that is passive about a mother's life. We're all about action, from the relentless cyclical progress inside us month after month to the anxious, sympathetic pushing we unconsciously perform beside our full-grown daughters as they strain to give birth to the first grandchild: Motherhood is all about the push, push, push.

Except when it's not. In a clamorous world that routinely mangles women's fertility when it's inconvenient, then tries to force her wounded body to conceive, there is a great need for simple receptivity — for openness, for women who are willing to say, like Mary, "Yes, I accept."

This is something that all mothers must do.

First let's talk about how it begins, at the very moment of conception. The egg moves into her appointed space, and then the sperm show up begging, "Mother, may I? Mother, may I?" After a moment's thought and some careful assessment, Miss Ovum nods to one, "Yes, you may."

Does the egg know what she is in for? Certainly not; and things may, in fact, go terribly wrong. But neither will she benefit from protecting herself, keeping inviolate, waiting around until she is sure. She will wither up and die if she refuses to receive this intrusion — that is how she was made.

And that is what receptivity is all about: making the active choice to let something happen to you, because you firmly believe that God had something in mind when he made you as you are. There's nothing passive about it. It takes a tremendous amount of courage to stand your ground and to say, "Let it be done to me."

Modern women are in pitched battle with their own fertility, because they perceive openness as helplessness, as victimhood. But it's vital to realize that motherhood is a vocation — literally, a calling, one that demands an answer. Answering "no," trying to sabotage that design, is what diminishes womanhood to a dark, cramped, inherently sexist biological state. We are designed in body and soul to say "yes" whenever we can, and in this affirmation of our nature is our strength.

A receptive woman is the most powerful creature in the world, in her deliberate openness: without her "yes," nothing more can happen. Life comes to an end.

Here's the tricky part: "Yes" can come in many different forms. Sometimes we say, joyfully or in tears, "Yes, I will accept another baby." But sometimes the fitting answer is, "Yes, I accept the need to put off a pregnancy right now." Or even, "Yes, I see that God will not give me a living child." Sometimes we stand there, open and accepting, and God comes to fill our cup with suffering. And still we must say "yes."

Does receptivity still sound passive to you? We must, in our openness, be made of steel.

Here are some ways that women must learn to be receptive:

◆ Accepting the physical pain of childbirth, breast-feeding, and the daily, thankless labors of caring for a family, because it's all *for* something.

◆ Being open to change, in ourselves, in our circumstances, and in the people we love. Learning to live with disappointment.

◆ Being patient with ourselves, our marriages, and our own spiritual growth.

◆ Allowing ourselves to be taken advantage of by the needy, especially by young children — because they need to learn not only gratitude, but also mercy, patience, and generosity.

♦ Allowing our children to get hurt, because that is the only way they will learn.

♦ Letting Daddy and the kids play that dangerous, unhealthy, unsanitary game that gets them all riled up before bedtime, because a mother's care is only half of what children need.

♦ Accepting interruptions, even from important tasks.

♦ Accepting loneliness and boredom, because even meaningful vocations don't always *feel* fulfilling.

♦ Accepting advice from more experienced women without taking it personally.

♦ Accepting help when we fail.

♦ Allowing ourselves to be misunderstood by people who don't value what we do.

♦ Deciding to trust someone who has let us down before, because trust makes people strong.

♦ Trusting that what happens now is not our fate forever: good and bad may both be fleeting. Allowing ourselves to enjoy what we know we cannot hold onto: the dimpled knees of a baby in the bath, the puppyish affection of a son who will soon be too cool to hug us. And fertility itself.

♦ Listening to the inner voice that says, "This is not just a normal fever — something is wrong."

- Listening to the inner voice that says, "This is not just a sulky teenager — something is wrong."

- Listening to the inner voice that says, "This is not a normal part of marriage — something is wrong."

- Listening to the inner voice that says, "This is wrong — but this is how it's going to be, so be gracious and loving even if no one else will."

- Listening to the even quieter voice that says, "Be still and know that I am God."

These are some of the many ways a woman can, in her strength, be open. Receptivity isn't passivity — receptivity is strength.

A Mother Is Creative

I know what you're thinking: *but I don't even own a glue gun!* When American women think of creativity, they think of the ability to do adorable things with baskets, or a flair for turning ordinary cake mix into an edible Advent calendar that synthesizes the Old and New Testaments in fresh and yummy ways.

That's not the kind of creativity I'm talking about. That kind of thing is lovely, but it's a talent, not a virtue. Not everybody needs it, anymore than everybody needs to be a gifted violinist or a whiz at math. Motherly creativity is something that is within the grasp of every woman, and you don't even have to buy a special kind of glue.

First, let's look at the word *creative*. In the most literal sense, only God himself is creative: He makes something out of nothing, out of the fullness of his love. We can't do this. But what we can do is to take very little and make it into something worthy of love.

Now, let's look at a mother's body. Eggs are produced every month, and sperm are a dime a dozen. On their own, they are mute and latent, trapped in the holding pen of potentiality. And they are designed to degrade and die, to turn back into nothing — unless they find a place inside a mother.

Once they find that place, it's Go Time. You can almost hear the cartoon explosions when the circumstances are right: POW! CONCEPTION! ZAM! GESTATION! Things begin to happen. The microscopic raw materials become something brand new, wholly irreplaceable: a human being with unique DNA; minute nerve endings; a tiny, tender set of femurs; eyebrows; a whorl of hair. And a soul. You can't make this stuff up. From zero to personhood in an instant? Forty short weeks to a whole new baby — are you *kidding* me?

And that's what I mean by creativity: I mean taking very little and making it into the most important thing in the world: human life. I mean using all your skills, anything you can lay your hands on, and making it into something good.

Now, our choices in this project of life are limited. When two lines appear on the pregnancy test, we're free to arrange for names and clothes and college funds, but it's not as if we can arrange for a wavy-haired athlete with delicate ears who has a taste for baroque music and eating dandelions. No mother in her right mind says, "I'll take lots of vitamin B and do prenatal ballet so that this baby will be tall, pious, generous, and resistant to bees." We can nurture this project along, but we can't completely control it.

It's the same for the rest of child-rearing. Raising a child is the most creative task there is, but it's unlike any other because, just like during the pregnancy, much of the process happens in the dark. You don't really know what you're doing. You can plan, you can try, you can respond, follow the rules, do the research, provide all the opportunities, and you can pray your brains out for your kids — but the finished product always gets away from you in the end.

I pray for two things for my children: that they will stay close to God (or keep returning to him), and that they'll stay close to each other. That's it. I want more, of course: I pray for happiness, success, good health, peace, and bounty. But I know that they can do without these things. They cannot do without love. If I can provide love, and put them in Love's way, then that's a big enough task.

So most days, I don't feel creative. I don't feel like turning ordinary sandwiches into whimsical, smiling faces that tempt the picky eater. I don't feel like transforming anyone's bedroom into a magical fairyland. Some days I can barely make it to the laundry room, so I certainly don't feel like making anything else.

But I do wake up each day and remind myself that this — these children, these boogery babies and smirking teenagers — *this* is what I'm making today. This is my project. If that doesn't sound creative to you, then you haven't seen the raw material I have to work with.

If charity believes all things, then creativity sees all things. A mother sees promise where everyone else sees nothing, or chaos, or a hopeless mess. Here are some ways that mothers can use their creative powers to turn very little into something that will glorify God:

- ◆ Bringing order out of chaos. Turning a wasteland back into a livable living room. Making an adequate meal out of odds and ends. Making a happy childhood out of a tight budget.

◆ Recalling people to their best selves during moments of pettiness: "Yeah, your brother is a stinker, but admit it — you love him."

◆ Feeding people's minds: pouring songs, stories, and ideas into little ears, knowing they won't remember or be grateful for this nourishment. And nourishing older people who ought to be grateful, but aren't.

◆ Feeding people. Just literally. The world needs to be fed, and sometimes only mothers remember how important it is.

◆ Recognizing innocence: realizing that Mr. Unappealing is shy, not snobbish; needy, not obnoxious; clumsy, not malicious; wounded, not angry.

◆ Encouraging virtue, even in its immature forms: no snickering when the seven-year-old adds, "the soul of the guy who invented Godzilla" to the family Rosary intentions.

◆ Quietly facilitating creative acts: filling out forms, doing the prep work, and cleaning up afterward so that *other* people can get projects done.

◆ Encouraging the unwilling. Some mothers are gentle and persuasive, some are bracing and demanding; but motherhood means you don't turn your back even on people who think they can do without your help.

◆ Recognizing gifts that don't look like gifts. My two-year-old told me, "Mama, I picked you some berries, and I ate them!" I thanked her most sincerely because I heard what she was really saying: "*I love you, Mama. I was thinking about you. And I like berries!*" Oh, those berries tasted sweet, even though they never made it to my lips.

♦ Praying. Praying. Praying. Mothers get tired, burnt-out, discouraged, distressed. Taking a midmorning nap or saying, "No, I can't do this for you" — these are parts of motherhood, too. We, like our children, are works in process, and God wants us to care for ourselves as well as for others. Sometimes it's time to stop working. But no matter how tired we are, there is one job that will always be ours: to pray.

A mother is creative. She is the one who keeps working when the rest of the world says, "We're done."

It's Terrible but True: A Mother Is to Be Left

To a pregnant woman, this is good news: that last trimester is sheer misery, and the moment of delivery is sheer relief. When we're finally in labor, we just want that baby out! Everything in us is utterly bent on getting it done, getting the baby out, letting him go, making it happen.

When the baby is born, friends and family say "hello" to that bewildered little face for the first time. But a mother, in the midst of the commotion and glorious release, also says a kind of goodbye: after sharing space and warmth, food and oxygen for nine months, that uncanny intimacy is finished, and two new individual lives begin.

The birth is glorious. But remember how it hurts.

Hello and goodbye — pain and relief, and pain again. This overlapping round song runs through the life of a mother: *Move along, move along…Why are you leaving me?* Just as our uterine muscles contract and push, the nature of motherhood is to coax, prod, and sometimes shove the children along, out into the light and away from us, away to something new. And, yes, it hurts.

It hurts because every used-up cliché of motherhood cuts us to the heart in real life — when baby's little purple overalls are indisputably too small; when we decide, "It's time for this child to be weaned"; when we drop them off at school and drive away with a quiet, empty car.

Rationally, there is no reason to cry — but sometimes we do, even as we're thrilled with the extra time and space, and pleased to see our little ones growing, learning, taking nourishment from someone else for the first time, just as they should.

In labor and in life, the way to bear the pain of delivery is not to fight against it, but to breathe, to relax, to be mindful of what is happening to us, and to help it happen.

This method does not actually work very well. At least, it doesn't take the pain away. But it does help the baby through. It turns the pain into something productive, something worthwhile, and not just something to survive. Hello, pain; goodbye, panic.

True for childbirth, and true as long as our children live. This is because to be a mother is to be two people — a mother's soul is not solitary. Our constant task is to care for our children, but to be willing to let go: to understand that we become more ourselves when we allow ourselves to be divided, from our children and even from our notions of who we are. Every time we give up something we thought we knew, we become more of who we are supposed to be.

Women can be astonishing stoics when dealing with personal pain — but seeing our children suffer? Unbearable.

There is double the anxiety, double the helplessness, and double or triple the guilt when we know we haven't prepared them well. And yet it must happen.

Here is where I find it easiest to turn to Our Lady: in suffering. We don't know what it really felt like for the Immaculate Conception to raise the Incarnation, but one thing is clear: Mary suffered because she loved her Son. That's just what being a mother is like.

Mary's arms are strong enough to carry all of her children, including us. When our children turn away from us, when they're physically or emotionally sick, or when they're mired in sin — when we see that we've failed, that we can't or won't do what we need to do for our kids — then this is when we say, "We both need a stronger mother, one who does not get tired of offering help." Goodbye, inexhaustible supermom; hello, Mary.

Once I was fearful, anxious, guilty, and desperately wanted that flowery Marian solace that so many Catholics enjoy. In great need, I looked at the rose-bedecked statue and thought in frustration, "Who *are* you, anyway?" And I heard the words, "I'll tell you who I am. I'm someone you can leave your kids with."

ᔕᔓ

I looked at the rose-bedecked statue of Mary and thought in frustration, "Who *are* you, anyway?" And I heard the words, "I'll tell you who I am. I'm someone you can leave your kids with."

ᔕᔓ

I had thought she would make me stronger; instead, she took my burden away for a time. She let me know that what I feared is true: I'm *not* good enough. She let me know that I don't have to be. Hello, weakness; goodbye, paralyzing guilt. Hello, motherhood.

A mother is to be left. We receive children, we care for them, and then we let them go. We look carefully at our own lives, we strive to be better, and then we let it go.

Here is what we can learn from motherhood, with its pain and its purpose — with its simultaneous "hello" and "goodbye":

◆ Learning to turn physical, emotional, and spiritual pain into something productive.

◆ Accepting change as a necessary part of life and not the end of the world.

◆ Letting our children have their own interests and strengths without making them feel guilty about being different from us.

◆ Not being consumed with worry over things we can't change, including sins of our past, the unknown future, and matters involving the free will of others.

◆ Acknowledging and developing our own strengths and talents without denigrating women who are different. Peaceful mothers are content to know that God hands out talents and limitations as he will, and that tearing each other down doesn't make us stronger.

◆ Struggling with our own sins, while being merciful and patient toward people who also struggle.

◆ Adjusting our ideas of what our bodies are for when they show the signs of age and hard use.

- Putting aside unsuitable ideals when the moment demands something different. Naming and attending to our actual duties, not trying to live up to some glossy perfection that other moms present as their lives.

- Learning when we *must* focus on ourselves in order to be strong and healthy enough to do our jobs.

- Learning the balance of humility: neither "I'm too good to scrub this toilet" nor "I'm a worm and that's why I deserve this scrubbing brush"; but "Here's the toilet, and here am I: might as well do it right."

- Being at peace with our own limitations of time, energy, and ability.

- Forgiving our own parents: imitating what was good, correcting what was bad.

- Not running away from necessary battles. Or, at least, always coming back.

Hello and goodbye, dear children. Hello and goodbye, old self. If I am who I'm supposed to be, I'll remember that you are safe with Mary, if only I can let you go.

QUESTIONS FOR REFLECTION

1. Where do I get my ideas about motherhood—what it means, what it's really like? From family, friends, popular culture, mommy blogs? Do these voices encourage and inspire me, or give me unrealistic ideas, or make me feel dissatisfied?

2. How would I complete this sentence from my own future eulogy: "As a mother, she was always so _____." How happy am I with that word? What can I do to write a better story about myself?

3. The modern world doesn't think much of motherhood as a vocation. Have I let this disdain seep into my own attitude? Do I ever feel guilty or ashamed for having children? How can I help myself (and my family) learn to value motherhood more?

4. Giving birth is the quintessential hopeful activity: It's God's way of saying that the world should go on. What are some simple things I can do each day to renew this hope in my life?

5. If I could only ask for three things for my children, what would I ask? What can I do to help them gain these things?

6. Do I really believe that God knew what he was doing when he chose me in particular to be a mother to these particular children? How can I show God that I trust his plan?

Simcha Fisher is a blogger and freelance writer who lives with her husband and nine children in a shoe in New Hampshire. She writes about many things, but her children like it best when she writes about motherhood, because she's always nice to them for a good week afterward.

CHAPTER 10

Plugging In and Embracing Discipleship in the Twenty-First Century

By Barbara R. Nicolosi

"How many of you saw *You Don't Know Jack*?"

The group of fifty Catholic CEOs and their wives looked back at me and blinked. A lady near the buffet yawned. Somewhere in the back of the room, one hand went up, sheepishly. My point was nearly made, but I pressed on.

"How many of you have even heard about *You Don't Know Jack*?"

This time there were a few scattered hands. Not more than ten people altogether.

One graying but very fit owner of a brokerage waved his hand at me in disgust. "We're busy people," he said. "We don't have time for all the garbage Hollywood is spewing out."

Most of the heads in the room nodded. Some of them were visibly relieved. They thought maybe we were heading toward the assertion that it was a bad thing that a roomful of Catholic leaders were completely clueless about the most over-the-top pro-euthanasia production to have hit the air-waves in, well, ever.

After all, why should a group of devout twenty-first century disciples, coming together for some fellowship, prayer, and formation, care that a critically acclaimed HBO movie advocating doctor-assisted suicide had been nominated for eleven Emmy Awards and won two; had won the Screen Actors Guild Award for its A-list star, Al Pacino; and won a Golden Globe Award for Best TV Screenplay? Why should any followers of the Lord, busy praying and brooding over the state of their souls, trouble their lives with a movie lion-izing Jack "Dr. Death" Kevorkian while it racked up other awards from the Directors Guild of America, the Broadcast Film Critics Association, the Casting Society, the Television Critics Association, and American Cinema Editors, among others? Why should a good Catholic care or even notice that while our "culture of life" side has said nothing to the people of today about euthanasia, the folks on the other side are already sweeping the award shows for their efforts? Why should we care?

You Don't Know Jack isn't important as an artistic or criti-cal benchmark. It was really only so-so as a movie. In fact, in the last decade there has been a growing tide of projects pushing euthanasia, including the Academy Award-winning movie *Million Dollar Baby*, the 3-D James Cameron block-buster *Sanctum*, and TV shows such as *ER, Law and Order*, and *House*. The thing that makes *You Don't Know Jack* significant as a sign of *our* times is the way the whole entertainment industry has embraced it, heaping it with awards, calling it "brave" and "groundbreaking" and a new standard for, as the Golden Globe announcer put it, "the next civil-rights struggle." Despite the fact that we Catholics are blissfully unaware of it, the battle for the right to die when you want, and the right to kill those who should want to die, has not only begun but is far along.

The only question remaining is, Will Catholics do something to stop euthanasia in the culture this time around? Will we speak back into television, movies, books, music, and plays the Gospel of Life the way we didn't with abortion or homosexual marriage? Isn't this the kind of situation that Pope Paul VI meant when he said about the modern media, "The Church would feel guilty before the Lord if she did not utilize these powerful means"?[18]

I hope most of us agree that it was a bad thing when, in the throes of the Sexual Revolution turmoil, devout Christians pulled away from the world of mainstream media, art, storytelling, and music. We committed ourselves to a subculture of our making, and the results for the Church and the world have been stunningly unremarkable. Which Christian artistic effort of these last forty years will survive this generation the way the Sistine Chapel and Mozart's *Ave Verum* have survived? Have we used cinema — the primary story-telling form of our time — in a way that has caused our age to "see your good works and give glory to your Father who is in heaven" (Mt 5:16, RSV)? What would it look like for us to do twenty-first century discipleship another way?

How can we Catholic women, as the backbone of the Church and the family, bring our values and voices into this culture?

Doing Twenty-First Discipleship Another Way

> Ours is an age of global communication in which countless moments of human existence are either spent with, or at least confronted by, the different processes of the mass media. I limit myself to mentioning the formation of personality and conscience, the interpretation and structuring of affective relationships, the coming together of the educative and formative phases, the elaboration and diffusion of cultural phenomena, and the development of social, political, and economic life.[19]

Did you skip over that quote? Because if you did, as a twenty-first century disciple you really need to go back and read it. A couple of times. As a former actor and then a playwright and poet, Pope John Paul II understood well that art, stories, and media are crucial elements of a fully human modern society. His apostolic letter about the media, called "The Rapid Development," exudes much more eagerness than foreboding for new technology. It also includes essential points for a Catholic in the media age — that is, we need to adopt culture and media:

- ◆ for the formation of personality and conscience;

- ◆ for the interpretation and structuring of our relationships;

- for education and formation;

- to absorb and appreciate Culture;

- to aid in our social, political, and economic responsibilities.

"For the Formation of Personality and Conscience"

Twenty-four hundred years ago, Aristotle watched a lot of plays, saw how they impacted audiences, and then wrote *The Poetics*. A practical treatise about how to write good stories, the work is still relevant. I find that when a screenplay fails, it's usually because the writer ignored some of the great philosopher's basic notes. Aristotle's reason for helping storytellers came from his unshakeable conviction that it is impossible for men to live together in harmony without good stories. Stories are the preferred way that human beings learn. We grow from watching characters make high-stakes choices — characters we have taken to heart in something like love. Good stories create empathy in us and a horror of evil.

I have a lot of hope for the Millennial generation, because they continually demonstrate the ever-human passion for good stories. As they have come of age, they have consistently rejected so many of the banal movies that Hollywood has offered them, preferring to leave the cineplex completely rather than be fed the industry's slash 'em, blow 'em up roller-coaster rides masquerading as stories. They want more from storytellers than stale and formulaic comic book reworks.

Say what you want about the magical context; in the end, the astoundingly popular Harry Potter series is more like the classic tales of old such as *The Arabian Knights, The Brothers Grimm,* and the Arthurian legends with their depiction of good versus evil.

The wonderfully talented folks at Pixar are doing much better things for today's little consciences than Disney tried to do with kids in the mid-twentieth century. From *Finding Nemo,* this generation has learned that real love will manifest as a combination of protection and freedom. *The Incredibles* made a compelling case for the necessity of family and struck a big blow against the leveling propensity of the tired, politically correct twentieth century. *Wall-E* drew a stark warning about humans in the future who have allowed technology to render them slovenly and isolated. And each of the *Toy Story* movies shared wisdom about friendship, community, and what it is to be a grown-up.

In many ways, we are in the heyday of the kids' conscience-forming movie. Thank God. As moms, we have a lot of great options in the theaters and on DVD that we can watch and enjoy and then talk over with our kids. As a rule, kids love to watch movies with their parents. And don't let the deadpan faces fool you — even your teenagers want to go to the movies with you.

But we need more than good consumers. We need Catholic writers who have brooded well over what exactly would characterize a Catholic point of view in cinema and other art forms. What defining themes should we bring to the table that the world needs as much as the human values being handled so beautifully by Pixar?

Pope John Paul frequently spoke of the prophetic role of the arts. Catholics can help artists navigate the difficult challenge of creating stories that awaken people without violating them. When I was in my early twenties, I was forever changed by the movie *Romero*, which made me aware for the first time of the real suffering of the Church in other places. It made me ashamed of myself — in a good way. A disciple of the twenty-first century will be on the alert to promote projects such as *Romero*, and *Hotel Rwanda*, and *Schindler's List*, and *The Lives of Others*, and *The Hurt Locker*, and so many more that are telling hard truths that must be heard.

"For the Interpretation and Structuring of Our Relationships"

As with everything else, the Church only cares about media as a means to help us realize our destiny: to love God, to love others, and to understand ourselves in the light of those loves. As women, we are the engines of caring in the society, and so our approach to culture should reflect this same disposition.

Nowhere are twenty-first-century human relationships receiving more play than on the Internet. Pope Benedict XVI encourages this new development and notes that "there exists a Christian way of being present in the digital world,"[20] It's so much harder to set this kind of example — and to teach our kids how to do it, too — than it is to just lazily swear off the Internet. Pope Benedict goes on to offer some guiding principles for Catholic chat-rooming, blogging, and Facebooking:

> Entering cyberspace can be a sign of an authentic search
> for personal encounters with others, provided that attention is paid to avoiding dangers such as enclosing oneself

in a sort of parallel existence, or excessive exposure to the virtual world. In the search for sharing, for "friends," there is the challenge to be authentic and faithful, and not give in to the illusion of constructing an artificial public profile for oneself.[21]

When I hear believers clamoring to live in a simpler time, I want to say to them, "Really?!" It's 8 a.m. here in Southern California. I've already checked my sisters' Facebook pages to see what they are up to in Connecticut, Colorado, and Rome. Via email, I referred a young woman in Sydney, Australia, to a priest I know there who works with young artists. I met him virtually through an Internet chat group. Over my morning coffee, I have already surfed through my daily rounds of the ten top Catholic bloggers to see what my fellow disciples are brooding about today. I texted my husband to meet me for Mass and confession tonight after work. And in twenty minutes I'm going to Skype with a diocesan committee in Florida about an upcoming festival celebrating uplifting short films. And it's all okay! Better than okay, it's great! I'm sure a "simpler" time had its own charms, but technologically mediated transcontinental ecclesial and familial bonding wasn't one of them.

Anyone who is paying attention is seeing one theme constantly rehashed on the big and little screen. The awareness of it should keynote the apostolate of Catholic women today. Whether it's irreverent network shows like *Modern Family* and *Up All Night*, or wonderful offerings like *The Middle*, or YouTube videos about a community of wildebeests saving their baby from some lions, people today are brooding over the question, "What is it to be family?" Most of the appeal of Harry Potter and *Buffy the Vampire Slayer* and *Twilight* is not the occult, but rather the vision of community they offer for kids desperate to experience the same.

This topic is not going away anytime soon. For fourteen years I have been a judge of one of the world's top student film festivals. In the last few years my fellow judges and I have been joking wryly about the fact that seven out of every ten finalists for the awards are about one thing: dysfunctional parent-child relationships. The prophets of the Millennial generation want to talk mainly about this in the same way that twenty-year-old Boomers wanted to talk about liberation. Related questions playing out in the culture are: "What does gender matter?" "Why should I get married?" "What do kids really need from their parents?"

As Catholic women, daughters, wives, grandmothers, and moms, we have something vital and saving to say about all of these things. But we need to share our wisdom through the same media in which the questions are coming — stories, plays, songs, YouTube videos, web-based episodic series, and someday, I hope, highly produced studio features and TV shows.

We can't respond to a gut-wrenching episode of *Grey's Anatomy* about out-of-wedlock pregnancy with an op-ed piece in a local Catholic paper. To keep shooting so low is not to have a pastoral heart in this moment of history. It's being lazy, or cheap, or fearful, or indifferent, or anything else that has kept Christians irrelevant and silenced in the modern marketplace of ideas.

"For Education and Formation"

A few years back, I gave a speech called "The Church and Hollywood" at a Eucharistic Congress in Washington, D.C. Afterward, a woman in a denim jumper and her husband in a plaid shirt and khakis stood nearby watching me meeting and greeting. They clearly had something they wanted to say. Finally, the woman stepped forward and addressed me in an almost challenging voice.

"Our oldest daughter is eighteen. She has always wanted to be an actress. She's actually been cast in several local plays," she said.

The dad added with pride mixed strangely with embarrassment, "She has even been in a commercial on TV."

This was good news to hear. This is the kind of kid who might grow up to be on *The Today Show* someday to tell her millions of global fans why she loves Jesus. So I congratulated her parents: "That's wonderful. What's she doing now?"

The mother squeezed her husband's hand and held her head high: "We told her we would pay for her to go to college for anything but that."

I was still young enough in my career as pleader for the arts in the Church to shake my head in confusion. The dad set his chin and added the kicker, "Because we don't want her to lose her soul."

Mom's voice wavered just a bit, "She's going to be a nurse."

I thought to myself, "Great, so maybe she'll just lose her mind." Today, I would add: "And chances are she'll lose her soul too. And probably she'll end up resenting you as a bonus."

In his *Letter to Artists*, Pope John Paul reminds us that everyone is called to be the artist creating the masterpiece of their own lives. But then the pope goes on to assert that there are some people among us who have been given the particular gift and burden of artistic talent. These people will only find themselves and God in the embrace of what the pope calls "the demands" of beauty. They will be prophets and priests for the rest of us, taking on the sacrifice of their hours of practice, training, and painful vulnerability so that the rest of us can encounter truth.

In what the pope calls the search for "new 'epiphanies' of beauty," artists find their own reason to be. Emmy Award-winning actress Patricia Heaton (*Everybody Loves Raymond*) communicated this wonderfully in a speech, saying, "When I am on stage, it feels like church to me."[22]

It isn't just the Internet and 3-D cinematography and digital surround sound that are gifts to be nurtured by the Church of the twenty-first century. There is also the primary gift of the thousands of young artists whom God is sending to us, whose talent will form the substance of how we use those technological gifts. You may have, right now, in a bunk bed upstairs, a John Lennon who will one day sing a song that quells anger and soothes souls. That kid across from you, sullenly moving her peas around on her plate, could be the Charles Schultz or Walt Disney of this century, creating characters that make people laugh and thrill and know they aren't alone. Maybe, that five-year-old who amazingly can do every word and gesture right along with the Wiggles is going to be the Mary Pickford or Meryl Streep of tomorrow. As Pope John Paul II noted:

> Those individuals in the Church community particularly gifted with talent to work in the media should be encouraged with pastoral prudence and wisdom, so that they may become professionals capable of dialoguing with the vast world of the mass media.[23]

Dostoevsky said it: "Beauty will save the world." And as the world becomes less and less agrarian, beauty will need to be mediated more and more by human beings. In other words, you or your kids through your works of art might save the world. That means that nurturing artistic talent has an evangelistic component.

So that they can be prophets to their fellow kids and someday to the world, Catholic children need to be exposed in a very intentional way to great works of art and storytelling. Catholic moms will need to do some art studying so we know the good from the bad to share with our kids. Then families will need to make the sacrifices necessary to give children music and voice lessons and have them experiment with watercolors and Final Cut Pro, and play around with digital photography and the drama club, all until their area of talent starts to emerge.

But maybe they really aren't going to have artistic talent? It still won't be a waste. I promise you.

I have spent my whole life surrounded by the arts. One of my sisters is a professional opera singer. Another is a musician and painter. Three of us are published writers. We took piano lessons and sang in church choirs and were fixtures in high school and college drama clubs. I can't overstate the benefits of a life spent learning how to be good at some kind of art. The great philosophers noted that exposure to art leads to refinement of the soul. In myself and my family, I have seen a direct correlation between the arts and growth on the spiritual, intellectual, social, emotional, and moral levels.

A twenty-first century apostle is going to be someone who values the arts and who shows it by supporting artists with prayer, encouragement, training, and commissions. In an effort to fulfill our own prophetic vocation, a disciple today will have to make time for the development of her own artistic gifts. Before we set out to save the world, we should energetically and beautifully decorate our homes, our communities, our churches, everything. And then we will surely find that the world, starved for wisdom and beauty, will come to us and ask us "a reason for your hope" (1 Pet 3:15, NAB).

☙❧

It has to be regarded as a modern heresy that so many contemporary Catholics have bought into a reactionary posture of seeing themselves as apart from the culture.

☙❧

"To Absorb and Appreciate Culture"

Everywhere I go, Catholics tell me that they never go to the movies or watch TV. Invariably someone waves his hand dismissively and says, "It's all garbage." If only it were that simple.

But the truth is, it's not all garbage. Some of what you will find on television on a given night is very, very good. What about the amazing human talent shown every night on *This Old House* and *American Masters,* and *Iron Chef America*? Or the fun new ways of doing history on *American Pickers, Pawn Stars,* and *Antiques Roadshow*? And, yes, what about the long-suffering struggle for excellence and perseverance that are *American Idol* and *The Amazing Race*? How can anybody watch some of the amazing documentaries that are out there on the National Geographic Channel and PBS and the History Channel and conclude that it is garbage? It isn't. A lot of it is beautiful and important work.

The more common case today is of media that is very, very good in some areas and somewhat problematic in others. Any episode of AMC's *Mad Men* is like that: a weird combination of amazing acting, writing, and production values, all interjected with moments that objectify human beings through all the confusions of modern life. It's not all garbage; it's complicated.

Five-year-olds clamor for everything to be black and white. Discernment is predicable of spiritually mature adults. It takes patience to teach kids how to glean the good from the bad in media today. You have to talk to them about the strengths of the show and help them identify the erroneous suppositions in the stories. But if you teach your kids how to watch wisely, they will become teachers to their companions. Media discernment is part of what discipleship looks like today.

This is not to say that there isn't a lot of very harmful stuff out there on television and on the Internet and in the movies. We all know there is. This isn't a call for us to microwave some popcorn and soak in all the slime slithering off the Spice Channel. Of course not.

Serious Christians need to experience the cultural arena not as fans but as apostles. We should be brooding over today's art and stories as signs of the times, not simply absorbing them like sponges. We have to fortify ourselves spiritually, philosophically, and ethically, so that we can enter into the cultural climate the way a doctor enters into a hospital. If we shun the hospital because there is some sickness there, it means that some of the souls entrusted to us will die.

But here's the real rub: if we avoid the hospital, we will also die, because we aren't just doctors to the times, we are also patients. We need the divinely inspired prophecy that all the modern popes have assured us comes through the arts. Just as much as our pagan neighbors, we need stories to lead us to wonder, hope, and compunction. If, in an effort to be safe from the corruption of modernity, we cut today's stories out of our lives, we cut out the normal channel in which God helps human beings grow in psychological, emotional, moral, and intellectual depth and sensitivity.

It has to be regarded as a modern heresy that so many contemporary Catholics have bought into a reactionary posture of seeing themselves as apart from the culture. We spend all our efforts not making culture but warding it off, purportedly to try and make ourselves "safe" from the flailing around of the rest of the human race. As if the story of the times isn't our story, too.

Because Hollywood creates movies that make sex obscene, we don't want anything that explores sexuality at all in our stories and entertainment. Because Hollywood glamorizes evil, we don't want to allow the representation of any of the lures of sin and temptation.

Because Hollywood lazily relishes the use of vulgar language, we react by clamoring for silly, sentimental characters who utter sanitized expletives like, "Mercy me!" and "Aw, shucks." Because Hollywood relishes highly stylized and graphic violence, we people of faith turn away from any kind of drama where people die or bleed or do really bad things, the kinds of things that are the logical result of living in sin.

Flannery O'Connor called this kind of clamoring for the safe among the people of God "an overemphasis on innocence." Because we are the people who are supposed to know about sin, it is possibly as serious a sickness as the wallowing in darkness that the pagans do. We need to deeply reconfirm the conviction that being naive, clueless, and aloof is bad discipleship and has little in common with the wisdom of serpents and guilelessness of doves to which Jesus calls us.

We need to be more like Chesterton's great fictional detective, Fr. Brown. His long hours in the confessional had led him to be a man like Christ who, knowing "what is in the heart of men," solved murders by a combination of great compassion and grim understanding of the seven deadly sins. Years ago, this was articulated for me in a way that stuck. I was a novice in the convent, and I was shocked to discover that there was jealousy and malice among a couple of the sisters. I shared my horror with an old Italian nun who was stirring a big pot of spaghetti sauce. She listened to me and then scoffed over her shoulder, "Only fools are scandalized."

As regards the arts, Christians before us used to be made of sterner stuff. What is "safe" about lustful Dmitry's dream in *The Brothers Karamazov*, in which a child is starving to death in plain sight? What is safe about Flannery O'Connor's serial-killing Misfit? What is safe about Dante's blaspheming bishops stewing in the seventh circle of hell or the graphic mural *The Rape of the Damned* on the walls of the Cathedral of Orvieto? For that matter, what is "safe" about the Biblical stories of King David, the murdering adulterer; or the sexual abuse of Tamar; or the violent crucifixion of the Lord? Nothing. As C.S. Lewis said of our Master: "Aslan is never safe. But he is good."

"To Aid in Our Social, Political, and Economic Responsibilities"

The Church is always and ever a mother. And as such, she is eminently practical. She would have us be grateful for the role technology has played in freeing us up from mundane tasks so that we can be more available to the people of our time. I remember my mother saying often that the women's movement had done much less for women than the vacuum cleaner, the washing machine, and the microwave oven. This is not a time to morph into some kind of perverse blend of Catholic Amishness. It may seem easier, but it isn't holier. Again, our Renaissance pope, Pope John Paul II, said it with his usual exuberance:

> Do not be afraid of new technologies! These rank "among the marvelous things" (Vatican II, *Inter Mirifica*) which God has placed at our disposal to discover, to use and to make known the truth, also the truth about our dignity and about our destiny as his children, heirs of his eternal Kingdom.[24]

The Church has blessed all the technologies that allow us to communicate better, to be more responsible citizens, to run our businesses more efficiently, and to benefit from the thoughts and ideas of the ages. There is nothing to be feared and much to be celebrated in e-vites to parties or getting whatever you need fast on Amazon or finding 867 possible options to fly from LAX to JFK on Kayak. Be a fruitful twenty-first-century Catholic and multiply your online presences! Our challenge is to baptize the goods of technology the way Christians through the ages have always entered into culture,: finding what is good or neutral there and utilizing it for evangelization.

Conclusion

All of the modern popes have spoken of the media of social communications as gifts that can restore a "villageness" to the global family. The media can allow millions of us from every corner of the world to focus on areas of need and to participate in a mass sharing of ideas. It's almost too much to handle, the incredible gift of traveling through someone's cell phone to a revolutionary square in Egypt. Or watching a tsunami in Thailand through some unknown person's uploaded camcorder footage. It's almost too much to know within minutes that Gaddafi is dead and to see the moments of his passing with five billion other people. It's almost too much to be able to follow presidential hopefuls in every moment of every day for months and months, to measure their every word and expression. It's almost too much; but, God knows, it isn't too much.

Blessed Mother Teresa, as the consummate woman of her time, once looked all of us in the eye through a TV camera and said: "Do not seek for an easy life. Seek to be a strong person." Living as a disciple today is a complex process of sorting through millions of ideas, passing over some and promoting others. It can be as tedious and challenging as it was for Christian evangelizers of another age to have to travel across oceans in rat-infested ships. But we were chosen for this moment; and until the word from above comes down to head for the caves, we are charged to be yeast in this culture. We're not just supposed to be out there in the culture. We are supposed to be important in the culture. So, dear sisters in Christ, let's tune in, plug in, and "Go into all the world and preach the gospel to all creation" (Mk 16:15, NIV).

QUESTIONS FOR REFLECTION

1. Pope John Paul II often spoke of the prophetic and necessary role of the arts in a fully human life. Examine your own attitudes about contemporary movies, TV, literature, and music. Do you avoid these completely? If so, where do you go to meet the human and developmental need for stories?

2. Have you ever been profoundly impacted for the good by a movie or television show? Have you ever been awakened to some social or global problem through a movie? Which one and why?

3. If you have children, are you providing opportunities for them to develop their artistic abilities? Do you cultivate this aspect of their lives as much as their athletic interests? Name one thing you can do in your home right now to more fully engage your children in the arts.

4. Pope Benedict XVI said that "there exists a Christian way to be present on the Internet." What does that statement mean for you in your use of the Internet? Have you sworn off it completely or kept it out of your home because of its potential for harm? What are you doing to train your children in a healthy use of the Internet, including seeing its value as an instrument of evangelization?

5. All artistic endeavors — whether in music, the visual arts, or literature — involve good storytelling. Do you think a story has to have an overt Christian message to be good? What can you do to educate yourself regarding the elements of a good story? Could you start a women's group in your parish to discuss the arts?

6. *Mother Teresa exhorted Christians not to seek an easy life. It isn't necessarily easy to develop an appreciation for modern technology — movies, TV, the Internet — and for contemporary literature, the visual arts, and music. Is anything holding you back from engaging the culture through these media? What are your fears? What are your fears for your children? What is God asking of you in regard to developing this area of your life and the lives of your children?*

Barbara R. Nicolosi is a screenwriter, cinema professor, and the executive director of the Galileo Forum at Azusa Pacific University. She founded Act One: Hollywood and works extensively with young people starting out in entertainment careers.

AFTERWORD

Hallie Lord

Long before the contributors had submitted their chapters, I started to think about what I wanted to say in the afterword. It's not easy to wrap up a book that contains such wisdom from so many amazing women. Over and over, the words that kept coming back to me were:

"Be who God meant you to be, and you will set the world on fire."

Sound familiar? They're the same words Jennifer Fulwiler chose to conclude her chapter. At first I was surprised that we'd independently decided to use the same quote from St. Catherine of Siena; but as I thought about it, it made perfect sense. Ultimately, we seek to order, heal, and foster the individual elements of our life so that our entire life, as a whole, will better reflect the light of Christ.

As with our physical selves, when one element is ailing it negatively effects all the other elements. Soon we find ourselves experiencing a general malaise without really understanding why or recognizing the source.

Without a healthy sex life, a marriage will suffer; without a strong marriage, our ability to mother will be challenged; without a balanced approach to the single life, what we are able to give to our communities will be limited; and when our souls are depleted, we have nothing to give. Everything is interconnected.

My hope is that the chapters that you have just read will help you to examine the most important facets of your life and guide you in bringing balance to them. Not only is this essential if you are to contribute to the good of our world, but it's also your right as a beloved daughter of Christ. He wants you to thrive!

Of course, this doesn't mean that we will never be sick, that we will never faces times of aridity in our marriages, or that we will never feel confused about what God is asking of us. What it does mean is that we will order our lives toward prioritizing good health — spiritually, mentally, and physically.

When our bodies ail, we must honor them enough to focus on healing; when our relationships go through times of hardship, we must make time to restore them; and when we feel that we have nothing left to give, we must turn to our merciful Father and ask him to pour his healing grace into us.

Perhaps this goes without saying. In this fast-paced world, however, we often forget to pause. We push ourselves harder and harder until we burn out. I understand the temptation — we aim to give of ourselves to others — but how can we possibly set the world on fire if we let the fires within us smolder?

Pope John Paull II included in the opening paragraph of his apostolic letter *Mulieris Dignitatum*, originally part of the closing speech of the Second Vatican Council, this reminder to women everywhere:

> "The hour is coming, in fact has come, when the vocation of women is being acknowledged in its fullness, the hour in which women acquire in the world an influence, an effect and a power never hitherto achieved. That is why, at this moment when the human race is undergoing so deep a transformation, women imbued with a spirit

of the Gospel can do so much to aid humanity in not falling."[25]

Take a moment right now and send up a prayer. Ask God to show you the path toward a balanced, healthy life so that you may play the unique role he has given you in aiding humanity. Surrender yourself to him so that the fire of his love may transform you, and so that you may, in turn, transform the world.

Go forth and set the world on fire!

Acknowledgments

Many thanks to Cindy Cavnar, my inestimable editor, who poured herself into this book with patience, wisdom, and grace. To Danielle Bean, who has given me every opportunity and believed in me long before I believed in myself. To my parents, who taught me to reach for the stars. To Jennifer Fulwiler, who is my pressure-release valve and provider of joy. To Daniel, Jack, Sophia, Lucy, and Zelie, who inspire me day after day with their winsomeness. And to my husband, Dan, who is my rock and all the proof I need that God loves me.

Notes

CHAPTER 1

1   Second Vatican Council, *Dogmatic Constitution on the Church: Lumen Gentium,* 7, November 21, 1964, www.vatican.va.

2   C.S. Lewis, *Mere Christianity* (San Francisco: Harper, 2001), 226.

3   Second Vatican Council, *Dogmatic Constitution on the Church: Lumen Gentium,* 12, 13, November 21, 1964, www.vatican.va.

4   Pope John Paul II, *Mulieris Dignitatem: On the Dignity and Vocation of Women on the Occasion of the Marian Year,* 31, August 15, 1988, www.vatican.va.

CHAPTER 3

5   Edith Stein, *The Collected Works of Edith Stein, Self Portrait in Letters 1916-1942,* translated by Josephine Koeppel, O.C.D. (Washington, D.C.: ICS Publications, 1994), quoted from http://www.wf-f.org/StEdithStein.html.

CHAPTER 4

6   Karol Wojtyla, *Love and Responsibility* (New York: Farrar, Straus, and Giroux, 1981), 273-274.

CHAPTER 5

7   Second Vatican Council, *Pastoral Constitution on the Church in the Modern World: Gaudium et Spes,* 24, December 7, 1965, www.vatican.va.

8   World Youth Day, "Beatified at 19 Years Old," October 28, 2010, http://www.madrid11.com/en/noticias/338-chiara-luce.

9   St. Thérèse of Lisieux, *The Story of a Soul* (New York: Doubleday, 1957), 113-114.

CHAPTER 6

10   Régine Pernoud, *Women in the Days of the Cathedrals* (San Francisco: Ignatius, 1998), 250.

11   Pope Benedict XVI, *Meeting with the Bishops of Portugal—Address of his Holiness Benedict XVI,* May 13, 2010, www.vatican.va.

12   Congregation for the Doctrine of the Faith, *Letter to the Bishops of the Catholic Church on the Collaboration of Men and Women in the Church and in the World,* 13, www.vatican.va.

13   Ibid., 13.

14   Pope John Paul II, quoting *Gaudium et Spes* in *Mulieris Dignitatem: On the Dignity and Vocation of Women on the Occasion of the Marian Year,* 24, August 15, 1988, www.vatican.va.

15   The precise phrase I take from a speech that Pope Benedict XVI gave to civic leaders in Croatia on June 2, 2011. However, "the principle of gratuitousness" is discussed at length in Pope Benedict XVI's *Caritas in Veritate,* 34, 36, www.vatican.va.

16   Congregation for the Doctrine of the Faith, *Letter to the Bishops of the Catholic Church on the Collaboration of Men and Women in the Church and in the World,* 13, www.vatican.va.

CHAPTER SEVEN

17   C.S. Lewis, *The Four Loves* (New York: Harcourt Brace Jovanovich, 1960), 65.

CHAPTER TEN

18   Pope Paul VI, *Evangelii Nuntiandi: On Evangelization in the Modern World,* 45, December 8, 1975, www.vatican.va.

19   Pope John Paul II, *The Rapid Development,* I.3, January 24, 2005, www.vatican.va.

20   Pope Benedict XVI, *Truth, Proclamation and Authenticity of Life in the Digital Age,* June 5, 2011, www.vatican.va.

21   Ibid.

22   Patricia Heaton speaking at the Legatus Annual Summit, Dana Point, California, February 2010.

23   Pope John Paul II, *The Rapid Development,* III.7, January 24, 2005, www.vatican.va.

24   Ibid., IV.14.

25   Pope John Paul II, *Mulieris Dignitatem: On the Dignity and Vocation of Women on the Occasion of the Marian Year,* 1, August 15, 1988, www.vatican.va.